DDT

"WE KNOW HE WAS A CRIMINAL SCIENTIST WHO'D BEEN WORKING ON A GIANT ATOM SMASHER..."

THE LEGION OF REGRETTABLE SUPERVILLAINS

ISBN: 978-1-59474-967-4
Printed in China
Typeset in Futura and Plantin
Designed by Timothy O'Donnell and Molly Rose Murphy
Production management by John J. McGurk

Quirk Books
215 Church Street
Philadelphia, PA 19106
quirkbooks.com

THE LEGION OF

REGRETTABLE SUPERVILLAINS

FEATURING THE 50 STRANGEST SUPERVILLAINS IN THE HISTORY OF COMICS

THE LOOT CRATE EDITION

by JON MORRIS

QUIRK BOOKS
PHILADELPHIA

INTRODUCTION

WHAT GOOD IS A SUPERHERO without a decent supervillain?

It didn't take long for the first comics creators to ask themselves that very question. While the dynamic new literary genre of the costumed crimefighter was still cooling on the windowsill, the heroes' opposite numbers began to crawl out of the woodwork. Almost immediately, their ranks were tremendous and their variety seemingly limitless.

From the start, the narrative burden in superhero comics has always been on the bad guys. They need to outnumber and overpower the heroes, enact a variety of schemes to provide conflict, be alluring in their appearance and modus operandi, and—most importantly—put the heroism of the good guys into stark relief. Some supervillains have risen to the occasion, and their fame has grown as great as the heroes they battle. Lex Luthor, the Joker, the Green Goblin, Thanos, Ultron, Doomsday—these are household names among comic book fans, and even in the wider pop culture universe their renown is on par with their noble nemeses.

But those illustrious reprobates represent only the tiniest tip of the illicit iceberg of do-baddery. Within the pages of this book, you will find villainy's vilest runners-up in all their weird, wonderful glory. These are the forgotten fiends whose often brief, and frequently fatal, careers belie a degree of wild invention—and a peculiar appeal which oftentimes make the crook the more compelling character than the hero. It's not their fault that so many of these lurid lowlifes and repulsive rogues enjoyed only short and uncelebrated careers. After all, it's

the hero who gets all the glory, while the villain does so much of the heavy lifting.

Read on and you'll meet wild werewolves, sensuous snake women, and avaricious alien conquerors in abundance. Also waiting for your perusal are such wild wrongdoers as a bioelectric brainpowered baddie, a space wizard with a nose-full of lightning, and a villain with a chicken head, just to name a handful of evil's weirdest representatives. Comics fans will find a few familiar and beloved—if bizarre—bad guys, including a flying cyborg head, and a mobster turned gorilla.

As in the companion volume to this book, *The League of Regrettable Superheroes*, we use the term *regrettable* lightly. No matter the shape, size, or strategy of the four-color finks gracing these pages, every one of them had the potential to join the ranks of comicdom's icons of evil. It was only poor sales, inopportune timing, and occasional overshadowing from bigger baddies which consigned so many of these scoundrels to the scrapheap of comics history. Until now!

Read on and enjoy the colorful variety of the medium's most forgotten foes and oddball blackguards. You'll find your own answer to the question posed above—a superhero without a decent supervillain is just no good at all.

TERRORISM AMONG
THE CIVILIAN
POPULATION!
THOUSANDS OF HOMES...
IN A RADIUS OF TWENTY MILES...
TRAPPED...MILLING IN THE
FURNACE-LIKE STREETS...
OPEN THE
SEWER! IT'S
OUR ONLY
CHANCE!
hours...THE CRACKLING
SEETHES FORWARD!
STARTED TO
OUR POWER
FAILS FAST, DR.
VOODOO! WE
MUST RETURN
TO THE SUN!
WITH THE ENTIRE NATION IN
THE CLUTCH OF PANIC...
TANKS ARE USELESS!
THEY TURNED RED HOT
BEFORE THEY COULD
GET INTO RANGE!
THIS IS WAR AT
ITS UTMOST...AND
IT'S A QUESTION
OF HOW LONG
WE CAN WITH-
STAND ITS
HORROR!
RED BAND
COMICS
THE
BOGEYMAN
WILL GET YOU IF
YOU DON'T WATCH
OUT!
WOW
COMICS
FAWCETT MAGAZINE
JUNE
NO. 14
MARY MARVEL
FIGHTS MR. NIGHT
FOR THE
IBIS
the
Invincible
HE HAS COME, SPANN
4000 YEARS OF TIME,
FACE AND FIGHT THE
THAT BESET US IN TH
TWENTIETH CENTURY
THOUGH FORCES OF FA
POWER CONFRONT HIM
the Invincible, WIELD
AGAINST THEM THE M
OF THE IBISTICK, WAN
WHITE MAGIC, GIVEN
TO USE FOR THE GOO
MANKIND! BUT BLACK
ALMOST OVERCAME
THE ADVENTURE OF
"The HORRIBLE
HAND!"
TRUG, THE WICKED WIZARD, IS MAKING A STRANGE CALL....
WHAT
DO YOU
WANT?
ARE YOU CROWLEY
THORNE? MY NAME
IS TRUG, AND...
I'M MR. THORNE'S SERVAN
HE'S EXPECTING YOU!
COME IN!

PART 1

The GOLDEN AGE 1938–1949

WHEN SUPERMAN DEBUTED IN 1938, he launched the immense, florid industry of comic book superheroes. His colorful foes, however, came a little later. Originally, the Man of Steel's opponents were limited to corrupt politicians, oligarch industrialists, penny-ante gangsters, and the occasional force of nature. His immediate imitators followed suit, and superhero comics began their existence presenting a notably one-sided battle for justice.

By 1939, though, the Man of Steel was matching wits with the insidious Ultra-Humanite and a modest coterie of sinister scientists. Meanwhile, his caped and crusading buddy Batman debuted in his own title confronting a homicidal harlequin called the Joker. Within the space of a year, supervillains were as common to comics as the heroes they battled.

A hallmark of the Golden Age of comics is the era's limitless sense of invention. The entire genre was shiny, new, and utterly devoid of established rules. This was a rich playground for imaginative authors and artists, who were required by their editors to produce continuous grist for the comics-reading mill.

Vile ventriloquists' dummies, brutish space invaders, diabolical demagogues, disembodied hands, avenging opera stars, femmes fatales and murder-happy menaces populated every inch of newsprint four-color fantasies in those days. And even wilder opponents waited in the wings, with comics creators seeming eager to outdo one another with weird variations on the villainous theme.

It was an era when anything was possible, and every kind of villain—no matter how strange or unlikely—was given a shot at the good guys.

NOTE: Not all scholars agree on the exact boundaries of these comicbookdom epochs, but the debut of Superman is generally considered the big bang of superhero comics.

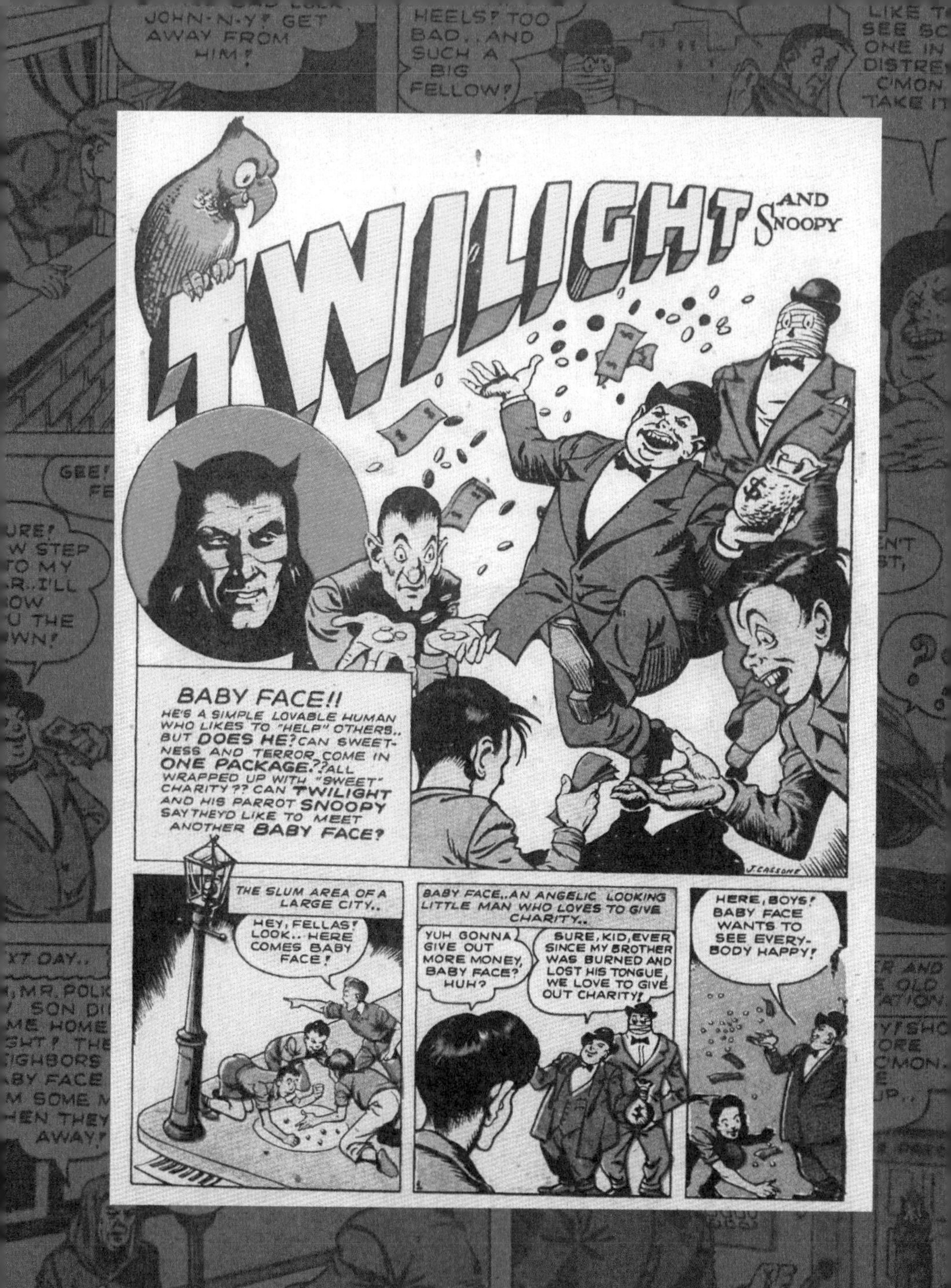

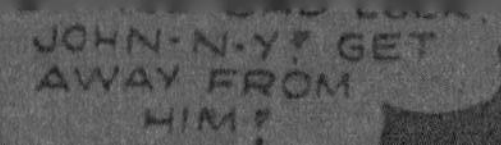
JOHN-N-Y? GET AWAY FROM HIM!

TWILIGHT AND SNOOPY
BABY FACE!!
HE'S A SIMPLE LOVABLE HUMAN WHO LIKES TO "HELP" OTHERS.. BUT DOES HE? CAN SWEETNESS AND TERROR COME IN ONE PACKAGE?? ALL WRAPPED UP WITH "SWEET" CHARITY?? CAN TWILIGHT AND HIS PARROT SNOOPY SAY THEY'D LIKE TO MEET ANOTHER BABY FACE?
J. CASSONE
THE SLUM AREA OF A LARGE CITY..
HEY, FELLAS! LOOK.. HERE COMES BABY FACE!

BABY FACE..AN ANGELIC LOOKING LITTLE MAN WHO LOVES TO GIVE CHARITY..
YUH GONNA GIVE OUT MORE MONEY, BABY FACE? HUH?
SURE, KID, EVER SINCE MY BROTHER WAS BURNED AND LOST HIS TONGUE, WE LOVE TO GIVE OUT CHARITY!

HERE, BOYS! BABY FACE WANTS TO SEE EVERY-BODY HAPPY!

BABY FACE AND BROTHER

"He asked for it, Brother. We are peaceful, but we can also be firm!"

CTS OF VILLAINY OFTEN hide behind acts of charity, and sometimes behind a bunch of bandages and a derby. That's the story behind Baby Face and Brother, a mismatched pair of apparent philanthropists whose freewheeling ways with fat wads of cash hide their sinister agenda.

VS

Plump and short-statured, his face contorted into a manic rictus of beaming joy, Baby Face is the derby-topped brains behind this felonious duo's complicated scheme. His so-called Brother, by contrast, is a hulking mute wrapped in bandages from head to toe. This is a pairing that cries "menace" from every pore, but they mask their unsavory auras by freely donating to the poor and distraught. "Ever since my brother was burned and lost his tongue," says Baby Face by way of unconvincing explanation, "we love to give out charity." Taking to the streets, the lugubrious Baby Face hands out thick stacks of dosh to the impoverished and underprivileged. Particularly beefy subjects receive extra attention. Lured by promises of further largesse or, failing that, manhandled by Brother, suitably poor and tough-looking men are shoved into a sleek sedan and whisked off to parts unknown.

These antics bring Baby Face and Brother to the attention of the superheroic Twilight and his partner, a wisecracking parrot who answered to the name Snoopy a good twenty years before Peanuts made the name a household word. Twilight was a curious crimefighter in his own right. The masked do-gooder was secretly Marine sergeant (and former wrestling champ) Terry Gardner. When trouble arose he would leap into battle wearing a T-emblazoned, fur-covered costume that left him looking like some sort of long-haired werewolf.

Twilight investigates Baby Face and Brother by disguising himself as a down-on-his-luck palooka. This requires pulling a lifelike rubber mask *over* his fur-covered cowl, the combination of which must have smelled like a floor mat at a pet salon. Taken to a secret dungeon where the abducted men are crammed into a tiny cage and abused by Brother, Twilight uncovers the full scope of Baby Face's evil scheme. It's a matter of revenge—*weird revenge.*

Brother, as it turns out, is no tongueless burn victim. Beneath his bandages and ill-fitting green suit, the titanic brute is a snarling, vicious gorilla! Twisted by hate after years of captivity, Brother turns the tables by torturing the captive men for his own amusement. "For years he was teased by silly people while locked in a cage," explains Baby Face, adding gleefully "Poke 'em with the stick like monkeys in the zoo!"

Enemies of:
Twilight

Created by:
John Cassone

Debuted in:
Clue Comics #5 (Hillman Periodicals, October 1943)

Not be confused with:
Baby and Brotherface

→

As for Baby Face, his desire for vengeance runs on similar fuel. “People poked fun at me because I was small,” he informs Twilight. For retribution, Baby Face carries a terrible weapon of his own invention: a reducing spray! “Now I’ll laugh!” he cries, demonstrating the spray’s shrinking effect on a helpless rabbit. But, in a subsequent scuffle, it’s Brother who’s struck by the shrinking formula. Enraged, the rapidly reducing ape turns on his “sibling,” brutally slashing Baby Face’s throat before being helplessly transformed into “a small, pitiful monkey.”

Freeing the prisoners, Twilight sums up the whole adventure adroitly. “What a weird sight,” he exclaims, standing over the twisted bodies of his former foes. “It all seems like a dream!”

ROLL CALL...

Other foes of Twilight included pedestrian menaces like Boss Bogus, the King of Counterfeiters, as well as more extravagant threats like the Porcupine, a hulking needle-covered beast referred to as “The Quilled Death!”

THE CAR SPEEDS OUT INTO WILD COUNTRY.. IT STOPS BEFORE A DREARY BUILDING..

AND "BROTHER"..WHEN YOU PUT TWILIGHT IN HIS NICE CAGE, RIP OFF HIS DISGUISE CLOTHES SO THAT WE CAN ALL SEE HIS NICE HERO'S UNIFORM! HA! HA!

TWILIGHT COMES TO...
WHAT IN THE WORLD IS THIS DUMP?..WHY! THEY'RE TORTURING THESE PEOPLE IN THE CAGES!!
HA! HA! THAT'S IT, BROTHER! POKE 'EM WITH THE STICK LIKE MONKEYS IN THE ZOO!

AND NOW IT'S YOUR TURN, TWILIGHT! HOWEVER, BEFORE WE SHOW YOU WHAT WE THINK OF BIG STRONG MEN-I WANT YOU TO MEET MY "BROTHER" AS HE REALLY IS...

AN APE!
YES..FOR YEARS HE WAS TEASED BY SILLY PEOPLE WHILE LOCKED IN A CAGE! NOW IT'S REVERSED! WAIT..I HAVE A SURPRISE FOR YOU-I'LL BE RIGHT BACK..

AS THE APE AND BABY FACE LEAVE, SNOOPY FLIES IN AND GRABS THE CAGE KEYS FROM A HOOK..
GOOD OLD SNOOPY!
CRAWWK! HERE.. NOW HUSTLE OUT!

THERE! IT'S UNLOCKED! OH,OH! DUCK,SNOOPY! HERE THEY COME AGAIN!

THE BALLOON MAKER

"After I have my lunch, I'm going to add you to my collection—and nobody will ever know!!!"

VS

Enemy of:
Frankenstein

Created by:
Dick Briefer

Debuted in:
Frankenstein vol. 2, #2 (Prize Comics, July/August 1948)

Primary characteristic:
Inflated ego

FRANKENSTEIN'S MONSTER (let's call him Frankenstein from here on out) is no stranger to comics. The iconic creature has appeared in dozens of incarnations in as many different titles. However, creator Dick Briefer's *Frankenstein*—once a creature of menace—enjoyed a second life as a humor character. And the now-pleasant and neighborly Frankenstein found himself facing villains of his own!

But horror elements continued to pop up, with the grotesque tale of the Balloon Maker as a notable example. His backstory begins when opportunistic explorer Hank Gallo stumbles across a peaceful African tribe that practices the gruesome but impressive art of skin stretching. Gallo exclaims in wonder: "This skin stretching takes the cake! Look! An ordinary pig—yet the skin is stretched out like a rug!"

It's true, the tribe has mastered a concoction that allows the flensed skin of animals to be stretched like rubber, and Gallo decides he must have it. Absconding with a twelve-year supply of the stuff, he's forced to murder the tribe's friendly leader as he escapes back to America.

Twelve years later, a parade, complete with colorful balloons, sparks inspiration. Before long, Gallo has set himself up as the greatest balloon maker of all time.

And, yes, those balloons are made of exactly what you think they're made of. Gallo might've gotten away with his horrific practices had he not impulsively hired the intimidating but avuncular Frankenstein as an assistant. On his way to his first day of work, Frankenstein stops at a carnival sideshow. There he learns from a weeping snake charmer that the attraction's stars have been abducted! They'd been last seen in Gallo's studio, *posing to have balloons made of them*.

Of course, Gallo has skinned the Fat Lady, the Tattooed Man, the Siamese Twins, and many more sideshow superstars, converting their stretched-out skin into dazzling, parade-ready balloons. He plans to do the same to Frankenstein, the snake charmer, and the carnival's "African Wildman," Bongo. But Bongo is in fact Bootra, son of the chief whom Gallo murdered. While Frankenstein frees the snake charmer, Bootra has plans of his own for the now-cornered Balloon Maker.

Later, back in his homeland, Bootra stands over his father's grave. "Mission completed," he grunts, "[I've] avenged your death." He gestures at a titanic balloon hovering above the burial site, a balloon resembling Hank Gallo.

YOU MAKE BALLOON FIGURES TOO, DON'T YOU? THAT'S WHAT YOU TOLD ME WHEN YOU GAVE ME THE JOB.
CX!!?X! I WAS HOPING HE'D FORGET ABOUT THAT! WITH THESE CARNIVAL FOLKS HERE I'M RUNNING A RISK!
ER--OH--YES. I'LL SHOW YOU!
YES..I DO MAKE GIANT FIGURES..IN FACT, YOUR FREAK FRIENDS POSED FOR THEM. THERE THEY ARE!
WELL, I'LL BE WOW!
WHY, THEY LOOK JUST LIKE THEM!! YOU'RE QUITE AN ARTIST, MR. GALLO!
YOU SEE, THEY'RE QUITE DIFFERENT FROM THOSE CLUMSY FIGURES YOU SAW TO-DAY. THEY WERE MERELY BALLOONS, BUT THESE ARE AUTHENTIC FIGURES OF ACTUAL PEOPLE, GREATLY INCREASED IN SIZE.. YET RETAINING ALL THE PROPORTIONS OF THE MODEL...
WHILE HE'S TALKING, I'M GOING TO LOOK AROUND!
8

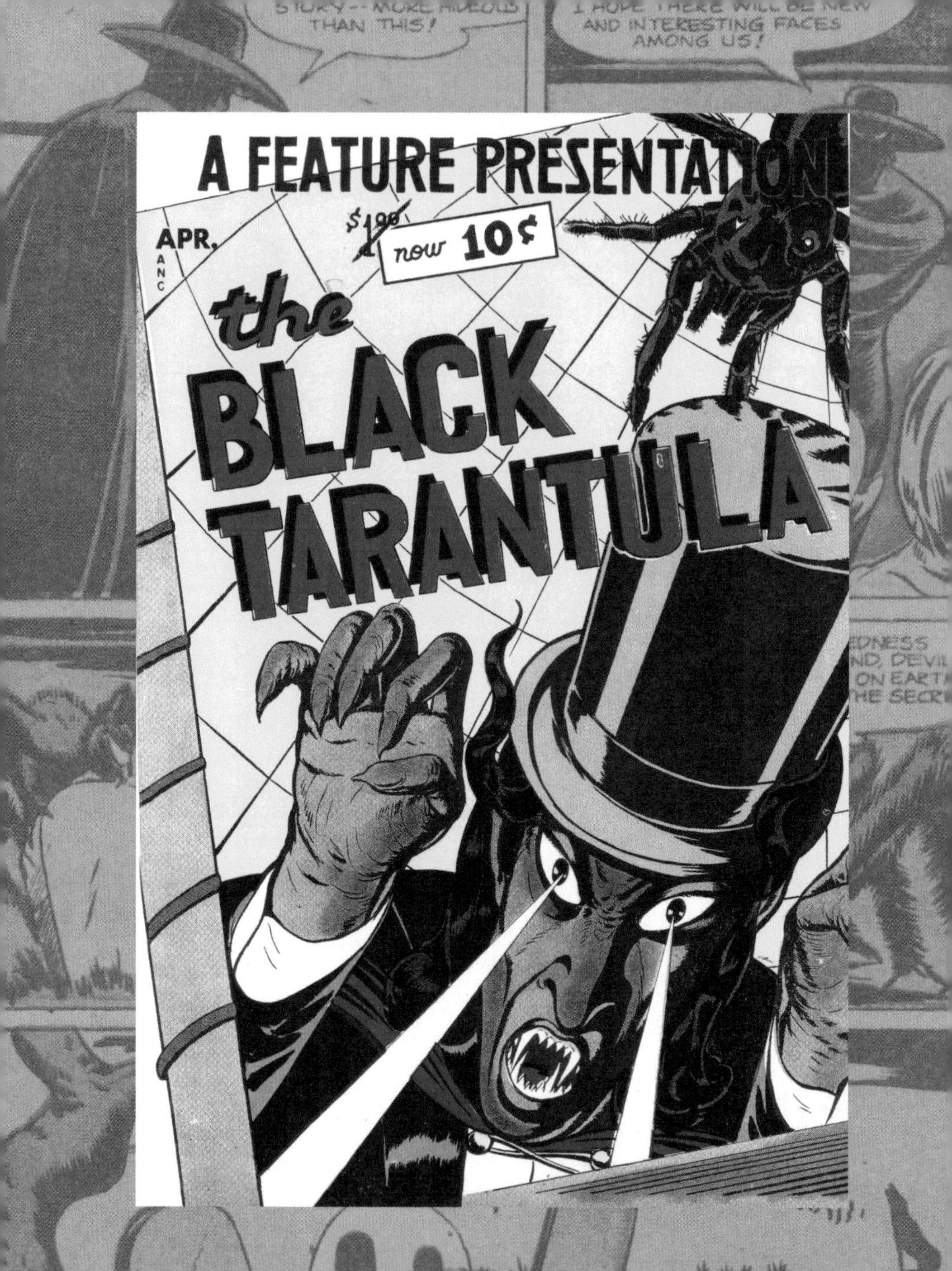

A FEATURE PRESENTATION!

APR.

ANC

$1.00 now 10¢

the BLACK TARANTULA

BLACK TARANTULA

"I go to spread evil and wickedness among you . . . while I am around, deviltry and cunning will remain on Earth!"

VILLAINS GET TO PLAY the long game. Whether their goal is world domination, the death of their greatest enemy, or the destruction of the entire universe, one thing is true: *they only need to win once.* Because of this, long-lived lowlifes and farsighted fiends have the luxury of letting their plans develop slowly over time. Sometimes, in fact, they set preparations in motion centuries before their goal. Such as in the case of the sinister Black Tarantula!

The Black Tarantula—or, I should say, *this* Black Tarantula, since the story makes mention of others—has lived for almost a thousand years when his tale begins. Hanging out above his own grave, he's delighted to direct our attention to his tombstone. It reads "Zoraster Rorret" (that last name is a real treat for anyone who reads their comic books in a mirror). The dates read "1101—[blank]." Gasp! "I laugh," explains Count Rorret, a gaping grin splitting his ghastly green face, "because there is no date of my death! How can there be, when I have eternal life? I'm dead, yet never will I die!"

Grim but merry contradictions like that appear to be the Count's stock in trade. Holding forth in a graveyard at midnight, he calls upon evil souls to share with them "The tale of ugly life and beautiful death, of evil good and good evil." The story details his seduction of the Princess Elthena: denied the liberty to wed her true love, a clean-cut commoner called Leopold, the princess chooses what Rorret calls "The happiness of death."

Becoming a titanic black tarantula, he bites her. This causes a living death which seems indistinguishable from life except for one dramatic change: the princess now finds "evil to be her only thought." Oh, and she can turn into a "hideously beautiful" and deadly black tarantula.

Terrified of losing his princess, Leopold accepts some tarantula bites as well. But it turns out that Leopold's grandfather was *also* a Black Tarantula. Therefore, Leopold knows that blinding a Black Tarantula robs it of its power! Granddad must have let that one slip at the family reunion. Leopold captures and blindfolds Count Rorret, despite the count's evil powers and demonic sidekicks (such as a pink-furred, amorphous, and size-changing creep called the Shape, who eats a few villagers before disappearing).

Leopold and the princess are happily married, while the Black Tarantula is entombed—for a while, anyway. In our century, he's free to follow up on his insidious plans. Or he would have been if he'd made it to a second issue. But if he waits nine hundred years, maybe Rorret will get another shot.

VS

Enemy of:
Princesses, villagers

Created by:
Unknown

Debuted in:
Feature Presentation #5 (Fox Publications, April 1950)

Favorite hiding place:
Behind a beautiful bunch a' ripe banana

BLOOR

"I am Bloor, dictator of Uranus. Take me to your ruler!"

VS

Enemy of:
Power Nelson, the Future-Man

Created by:
Paul Norris and Dick Sprang

Debuted in:
Prize Comics vol. 1 #4 (Prize Comics, June 1940)

Reason for the snickering:
Keeps saying he's the dictator of Uranus

THE WORLD IS HAVING a very rough time by the futuristic year of 1982, according to the story of Power Nelson, the Future-Man. To begin with, civilization has been conquered by "a Mongol horde," an invading force that otherwise hasn't been much of a threat to world peace since the fourteenth century. Additionally, it's the economy, stupid: the ultra-futuristic capital city of New New York is suffering an unemployment crisis. Riots have broken out, and the emperor can only make empty promises. It's during the peak of this crisis when a fleet of ships arrive from Uranus, bearing with them the leader of the distant world: Bloor!

Looking something like a deflated green air mattress dangling from a clothesline, or possibly a frog who got into a box of stick-on googly eyes, Bloor may not strike an imposing figure on his own. Once he gets a slave army back to his home planet, though, it's a different matter. But first he meets with Earth's cruel emperor and makes a tempting offer. It seems he has a labor shortage, needs thousands of men, and in exchange: "I have ten tons of gold for you!" The emperor is thrilled, and doesn't seem thrown when he asks Bloor what wages he pays, only to have the reptilian ruler reply: "Wages—BAH!!"

The Uranian ships, loaded with human workers, rocket back to the faraway world—where they're met by whip-wielding slave drivers. "You eat once a day. There is no pay day. You'll just work—and *like it*!" explains an overseer, identical to Bloor except for his garments of authority—a gold-scaled suit with a mask decorated with radiating fins. Uranus is a high-fashion planet.

Meanwhile, Power Nelson becomes curious about the legitimacy of Bloor's job offer and decides to check out the situation for himself. To put it in words that are fun to say out loud: What he sees on Uranus disgusts him.

Slaves are chained to their machines! It's forced labor! Smashing through the wall, Nelson breaks the workers' chains and prepares to meet Bloor face-to-face. Unfortunately for Nelson, Bloor is a middle-manager type: he does his fighting from the comfort of his desk. He summons his "Amazon regiment"—blonde-haired, light-skinned beauties in armor, vastly different looking from Bloor's pie-eyed, lizard-skinned people. Nelson refuses to fight the women, displaying the progressive gender politics of the 1980s. But when he's dragged before Bloor, he's happy to take a swing at the frog-faced fink. Bloor defends himself in the way he knows best: by pressing a handy button on his desk which summons giant robots to fight for him.

Nelson naturally makes short work of them, because they were male robots. →

— AND TAKEN TO BLOOR...
SO YOU'RE A STRONG MAN, EH? BUT YOU CAN'T TAKE IT!

I CAN'T FIGHT WOMEN, BUT —

POWER BREAKS HIS BONDS....
I CAN FIGHT YOU!

BLOOR PRESSES A BUTTON ON HIS DESK —

—AND TWO HUGE ROBOTS APPEAR...

POWER WHIRLS TO FACE THEM...
CAN'T DO YOUR OWN FIGHTING, EH?
15

So the still-seated tyrant decides to renegotiate his hiring terms. "The men from Earth are to be returned home with full pay!" he barks into his intercom, adding, lest anyone on Uranus doubt his authority, "These are Bloor's orders!"

EDITOR'S NOTE...

Although Bloor's allies—and Power Nelson's foes—are described as Mongols, they're clearly meant to represent the Imperial Japanese army of the era. The "Mongol" leader, Seng I, is an obvious caricature of Japan's Emperor Hirohito.

FOLLOW THE FIGHT OF **POWER NELSON,** *the* **FUTURE-MAN,** IN EACH ISSUE *of* **PRIZE COMICS**

SEE MORE NEW WORLDS WITH POWER NELSON—NEXT MONTH

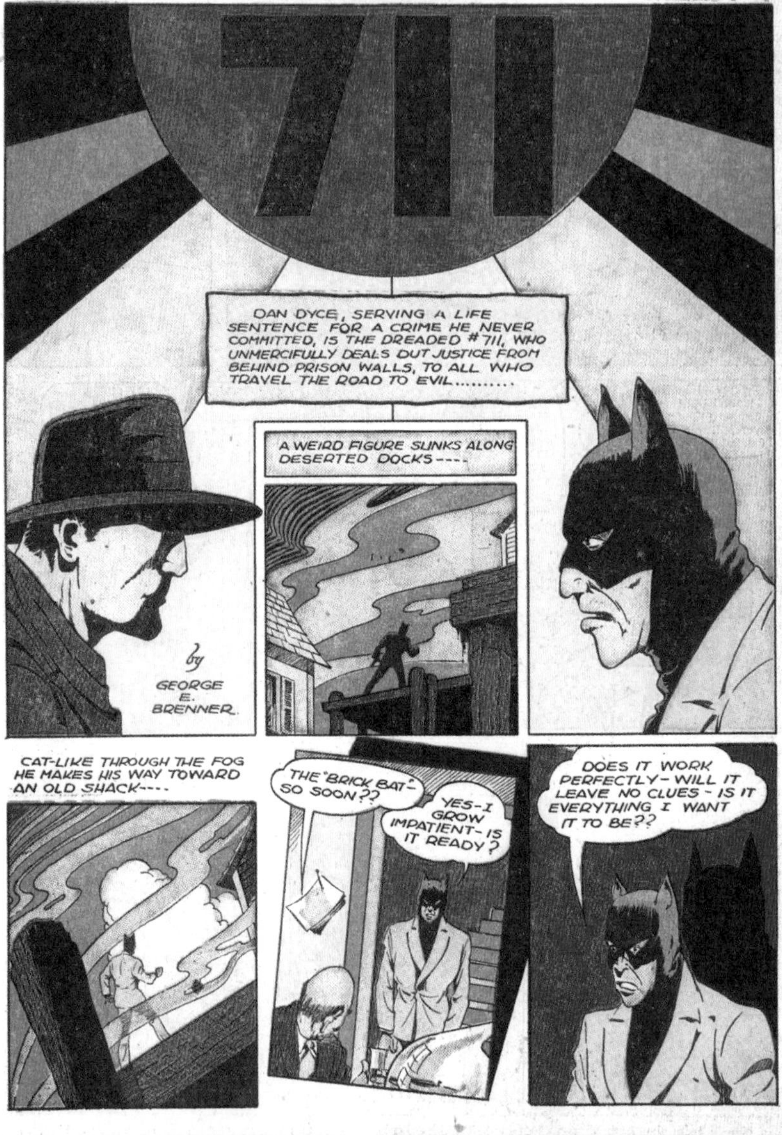

711

DAN DYCE, SERVING A LIFE SENTENCE FOR A CRIME HE NEVER COMMITTED, IS THE DREADED #711, WHO UNMERCIFULLY DEALS OUT JUSTICE FROM BEHIND PRISON WALLS, TO ALL WHO TRAVEL THE ROAD TO EVIL.........

by GEORGE E. BRENNER

A WEIRD FIGURE SLINKS ALONG DESERTED DOCKS----

CAT-LIKE THROUGH THE FOG HE MAKES HIS WAY TOWARD AN OLD SHACK----

BRICKBAT

"You're ruined and too old to recoup your fortunes—you're better off dead, fool—so die!"

ITH SOME SUPERVILLAINS, YOU find yourself pondering which came first: the concept or the name. Did the creator have a great idea for a bad guy and then build a *nom du villainy* to suit it? Or was inspiration sparked by an innocently uttered word overheard in idle conversation? With Brickbat, there's very little guesswork involved. "A crook who dresses like a bat and strikes his victims with bricks" is not a concept that exists independently of the word "Brickbat."

Liberally armed with bricks, Brickbat wore a bat-eared mask reminiscent of a much more popular crime *fighter* residing at a rival comics publisher. Lest confusion reign between the two blue-hued, pointy-eared cowls, Brickbat completed his outfit with a lime green blazer and slacks. Consider it the supervillain equivalent of the mullet: business below the neck, party up top. And pockets full of bricks.

Bearing on his person any number of gimmicked, breakaway bricks—each filled with fatal gas—Brickbat's M.O. was to rob his victims blind and then murder them by chucking the insidious blocks of clay and poison right at them. The bricks were the creation of an unnamed scientist whom Brickbat promptly murdered. (The science of gas-filled masonry has never recovered.)

Of course, it seems obvious that a regular brick would be a more useful weapon. For starters, you can use a real brick over and over again. With one-shot poison bricks, however, you have to carry a bunch around if you want to murder more than a single individual. And where exactly is Brickbat carrying all of his bricks? He seems to have several on him at any given time. Those green slacks must have deep pockets.

Perhaps the only advantage of fake bricks filled with deadly gas is that accuracy isn't much of a factor. But 711—an incarcerated superhero who escapes from prison every night to battle crime—finds a way around this. In their sole confrontation, 711 stands next to an open window as he taunts the heavy-handed crook. Enraged, Brickbat empties his entire quiver at the sanguine-suited superhero. And he misses each time, as 711 dodges and the deadly bricks "pass harmlessly through the glass." Hopefully, no one happened to be walking through the alley below that window.

Once Brickbat is completely out of ammo, he's subject to 711's sole superpower: punching crooks repeatedly in the head until they fall down. And Brickbat is committed to the same prison that holds 711 in his civilian identity.

Enemy of:
711

Created by:
George Brenner

Debuted in:
Police Comics #5 (Quality Comics, December 1941)

Not to be confused with:
Cinderblock Fox; Paving Stone Bear

COLOSSUS A.D. 2640

"I am the mightiest man in the whole universe!"

VS

Enemy of:
Dr. Blitzmann

Created by:
Reinsberg and Bernie Wiest

Debuted in:
Colossus Comics #1 (Sun Publications, 1940)

Earth shirt size:
XXXXXXXX
XXXXXXXXL

FEW SUPERVILLAINS HAVE STARRED in their own title, and fewer still did so in their first appearance. But the Colossus—or, more specifically, Colossus A.D. 2640—debuted against the background of a garish, lemon-yellow comic cover, crushing rocket ships as fancifully dressed soldiers fainted and ran at the sight of him. Whatever else you might say about him, Colossus knew how to make an entrance!

But first, we learn that the world of the far-flung future has its problems. Namely, alien invasion is imminent. "Plantaliens!" declares one witness, his eye pressed to a gigantic, brightly colored telescope, "invading the solar system again after 60 years!"

Meanwhile, one Dr. Blitzmann is unveiling his latest discovery: illegal steroids.

Blitzmann explains to strapping he-man Bryn Hale and, more importantly, to his hunched-over apish assistant, Richard Zenith, that he's created a glandular formula that controls human growth. A tiny injection, he says, will remake Zenith into the tall, athletic type he's always wanted to be, "like our colleague Bryn Hale." To save time, he injects Zenith with the drug before he finishes explaining its effects. Quite an ego boost for tall, athletic Hale, but a boost of a different sort for Zenith. Suddenly the doctor's daughter Eve rushes into the room. Whoops, instead of using two one-hundredth parts of the catalyst, she put 200 parts into the formula!

Soon the former lackey stands over 2,000 feet tall. With his new power quite literally going to his massive head, he announces, "Zenith is now Colossus, ruler of all the Earth!" The giant declares himself "God over puny mankind," and—after abducting Eve and zipping her in his inexplicably enlarged shirt pocket—sets about wrecking nearby cities. He shrugs off rocket attacks and blinks away laser blasts aimed directly at his eyes. He seems unstoppable . . . and then the Plantaliens finally arrive (remember them?).

"Blasted Plantaliens," Colossus roars. "Try to take over my property, will you!" A Plantalien ship crashes into Colossus's shirt pocket, from which Eve (with an assist from handsome, heroic, enviable Bryn Hale) had just a moment earlier escaped unnoticed (phew). Furious because he believes his hostage is dead, Zenith vows to make the invading fleet pay for this effrontery. Unfortunately, the sudden cancellation of the book precluded a part two of the tale. What would have come next is anyone's guess. But if the beginning of the story is any indication . . . it would have been big.

COLOSSUS COMICS

MARCH

10 CENTS

featuring

COLOSSUS a.d. 2640

Lucky Lucifer

TULPA OF TSANG

LUM SIMS

BLOND GARTH "King of the Isles"

AND OTHERS

200 FREE PRIZES

ALL NEW • ALL COMPLETE!

MR. SCARLET and the DEATH BATTALION
AS THOUGH BACK FROM THE GRAVE, SIX SINISTER CRIMINAL MASTER MINDS RETURN IN AN UNHOLY ALLIANCE TO PREY UPON CIVILIZATION! MERCILESS MURDER STRIKES FROM ALL SIDES, IN A COLOSSAL CABAL OF DEATH! BUT THE SAME CHAMPION WHO BEFORE SMASHED THEM, STRIKES BACK— MISTER SCARLET MAN OF MYSTERY....
IN EL CATRAZ PENITENTIARY ONE NIGHT, WHERE THE COUNTRY'S MOST VICIOUS CRIMINALS ARE BEHIND BARS.
JAIL BREAK!
CLANG! CLANG!
SHAKEN BY THE EVENT, AS SIX PRISONERS ESCAPE, WARDEN LOOMIS RESIGNS THE NEXT DAY.
I'M RETIRING. I NEED NOT REMIND ALL OF YOU THAT THE SIX ESCAPED MEN ARE DANGEROUS!

THE DEATH BATTALION

"Five key men are in the city tonight . . . who must die! With them gone, our Putsch for control of America is launched!"

NOT EVERY SUPERHERO CAN achieve the level of success and popularity enjoyed by the top-most tier of costumed crusaders. Then again, masked crime-fighting isn't always a popularity contest. Some heroes become fan favorites on the merits of their accomplishments—and the accomplishments of their enemies.

Take, for instance, the mystery duo of Mister Scarlet and his kid sidekick, Pinky. They didn't sport the most intimidating or inspiring alter egos (essentially, "A red guy and his slightly less red partner"), they didn't possess the most glamorous secret identities (Mr. Scarlet was such a successful crime-fighter that he put his civilian self out of a job as district attorney), they boasted little in the way of powers (both packed sidearms and Mister Scarlet could—sometimes, and with little explanation—fly), and their costumes didn't exactly instill fear in cowardly and superstitious criminals (unless the crook had a phobia of red suits with yellow capes).

What the pair did enjoy was one of the most expansive and well-populated rogues' galleries in the early days of comics. A few dozen twisted ne'er-do-wells, fifth columnists, and straight-up whacked-out weirdos made Mister Scarlet and Pinky their personal targets in the characters' otherwise underrated crime-fighting careers.

On one occasion, in fact, the duo was menaced by a baker's half dozen of their most wicked foes at once, in the form of the sinister Death Battalion. An agency dedicated to the assassination of top government officials, the weird menaces of the Death Battalion are freed from the otherwise-redoubtable high-security prison El Catraz (Spanish for "The Catraz"), by a mysterious figure. "As though back from the grave, six sinister criminal masterminds return in an unholy alliance to prey upon civilization!" cries the introductory caption of their debut. "But the same champion who before smashed them, strikes back—Mister Scarlet, man of mystery . . . "

For the most part, the members of the Death Battalion sport some pretty sinister sobriquets:

DR. DEATH: An evil concert musician, he composes a "symphony of death," which kills any musician who plays it (eliminating any possibility of an encore).

THE GHOST: An embezzler who robs the charitable orphanage fund on the board of which he serves, he's aided by a gang dressed in terrifying ghost and skeleton costumes.

THE HORNED HOOD: This criminal mastermind was a respected scholar in his →

VS

Enemies of:
Mister Scarlet and Pinky

Created by:
Otto and Jack Binder, Don Rico

Debuted in:
America's Greatest Comics #1 (Fawcett Comics, September 1941)

Not to be confused with:
The Murder Brigade; The Near-Death Experience

civilian alter ego. By night, he became a feared jewel thief, armed with a lethal, lead-filled club of thorns.

THE BLACK THORN: A hooded fifth columnist who armed himself with the Mummy Ray, a device that could fatally dehydrate his enemies at the flick of a trigger. That's pretty good, but you know he had his eyes on the Horned Hood's thorn club.

THE BLACK CLOWN: Armed with the skills of circus performing—watch it, he's got a unicycle!—he was aided in his evil schemes by assorted circus professionals, including a vicious gorilla named Garganta.

THE LAUGHING SKULL: This skull-masked disgraced banker forced his enemies to read their own epitaphs before murdering them at their grave sites.

The Battalion was organized by a figure in a mesh helmet who called himself the Brain, and proved to be none other than the warden of El Catraz prison. His not-at-all-half-baked plan to unleash these various villains from incarceration in order to overthrow the United States government starts off promisingly. But Mister Scarlet and Pinky, whatever their other qualities, make short work of the felonious fiends. It certainly can't have been good for the Battalion's confidence to find their plans overthrown by these consistently underrated superheroes. Perhaps that's why the group never reformed—in either sense of the word.

ROLL CALL...

Among Mister Scarlet and Pinky's other foes were the murderous Mister Hyde, the musical hitman called the Hummer, a modern-day Bluebeard, the hulking Boss, the mysterious Moon Torchman, the arson-happy Fire Fiend, the Hook, the Voice, and an unseen figure called Mr. Nobody . . . who turns out to be a secret crime-fighter himself!

AND THAT SAVES THE LAST VICTIM! NOW TO RAID THE BRAIN'S LAIR FOR THE SHOWDOWN!
BOY OH BOY OH BOY!
MEANWHILE, AT THE LAIR OF THE BRAIN, THE BLACK CLOWN AND GHOST REPORT.....
SCARLET STOPPED ME FROM GETTING KUDSEN!
AND HIS BRAT, PINKY INTERFERED AT DOOVER'S PLACE!
SCARLET! SCARLET! THAT'S ALL I HEAR! WHERE ARE HORNED HOOD AND LAUGHING SKULL?
NOT HERE! SCARLET MUST'VE GOT THEM!

BUT THE TWO MISSING MEMBERS OF THE DEATH BATTALLION ARRIVE.
THERE YOU ARE!
WE GAVE SCARLET THE SLIP!

STUPID DOLTS! NOW WE HAVE TO LAM FOR A NEW HIDE-OUT!
LET'S GO BEFORE SCARLET ARRIVES!

GOING SOMEWHERE, GENTS?
WE TOOK THE PLACES OF LAUGHING SKULL AND HORNED HOOD!

THE TWIN RED CRIME-BUSTERS EXPLODE INTO ACTION AGAINST THE DEATH BATALLION!
PRETTY SOMERSAULT, BLACK CLOWN!

THE DICTATOR

"You stupid offspring of a pig!"

VS

Enemy of:
Mr. Justice

Created by:
Joe Blair and Warren King and/or Sam Cooper

Debuted in:
Blue Ribbon Comics #13 (MLJ Publications, June 1941)

Not to be confused with:
Bloor, dictator of Uranus (see page 20)

THROUGHOUT THE 1940S, superhero comics were rarely shy about making direct associations between Adolf Hitler and any variety of vile monsters or criminals. Dozens—and possibly hundreds—of saboteurs, gangsters, traitors, and even infernal creatures either took direct orders from the Führer or were in some fashion partnered up with him and the Nazi cause. However, no other villain took that connection to quite the same extreme as the Dictator—who was a literal combination of both Hitler *and* Satan!

"A nameless thing of evil looks down on a world erupting with hate and greed," explains the Dictator's introductory text as a leering crimson-skinned figure stares from his throne of skulls upon a smoking model of the Earth. "And in the thing's foul and distorted mind, a vicious plan takes form . . . "

Transforming himself into an anonymous housepainter, the Dictator goes to work. He spreads a "gospel of evil and terror," turning a nation into an armed camp and threatening world peace with escalating militarism.

Confronting the Dictator is Mr. Justice, the avenging spirit of an unjustly murdered eleventh-century English prince who returns to battle evil in the modern day. A fiend as high profile as a combination Hitler/Devil couldn't possibly escape the notice of a dedicated crime fighter like Mr. Justice. "That man and his fanatical lieutenants must be stopped before they destroy civilization!" he observes, further pledging that "The time is ripe to stop ignoring the dictator . . . and do something about him!"

And do something he does! Mr. Justice clashes repeatedly with the Dictator over the course of more than a half dozen consecutive issues, striking at the menace's support structure of vain, power-hungry lieutenants and marshals. After all, he deduces, the Dictator can exist in mortal form only because he's supported by evil men.

In time, the Dictator withdraws from direct confrontation with Mr. Justice, choosing to send magically enchanted subordinates such as the Evil Eye and the titanic Green Ghoul.

The Dictator's choice to delegate authority undoubtedly helped Mr. Justice's crime-fighting career. Although a concatenation of the supernatural incarnation of all evil and the political leader of the Western world's most aggressive military dictatorship might make for the most capital-V Villain in the history of comics, it does limit a hero's options. Whom do you battle when you've already taken on a dual-purpose Devil/Hitler?

MR. JUSTICE
by
S. COOPER
LL EUROPE ECHOES WITH THE RUMBLING THUNDER OF THE MARCHING ARMIES OF THE DICTATOR--BUT ONLY MR. JUSTICE KNOWS THAT THE DICTATOR IS, IN REALITY THE EPITOME OF ALL THINGS EVIL!... AND HE HAS RESOLVED TO DEFEAT THE MONSTROUS THING BY FIRST DESTROYING THE MILITARY JUGGERNAUT WHICH SUPPORTS HIM AND HIS REIGN OF BLOOD AND TERROR!

DAREDEVIL
SILVER STREAK COMICS
$100.00 PRIZE-WINNERS ANNOUNCED IN THIS ISSUE!
10¢ DECEMBER No.17
The great, the one and only
CAPTAIN BATTLE
and his courageous young pal
HALE
are called upon to free the nation from Nazi plotters in a new hideous form. With unequaled bravery, the mighty pair tear into the foeman with flaming fury. SEE PAGE 11
★ SILVER STREAK AND METEOR ★
★ DICKIE DEAN ★ DAREDEVIL ★
★ PRESTO MARTIN ★ PIRATE PRINCE ★
★ and Others. ★ Every One a Lead Feature!
BINDER

DR. DRACULA

"The death ray will conquer the world! I, Dr. Dracula, will be governor of America!"

OMIC BOOKS LOVE THEMSELVES a Dracula. This explains the abundance of characters bearing that moniker, from the original bloodsucker to any variety of pretenders—both heroes and villains—using the Dracula name or variations thereof. When it comes to Dr. Dracula, however, the use of the appellation raises more questions than it—or the story in which he appears—answers. Did this character merely append "Doctor" to his already ominous family name to lend it an additional air of menace? Or is he a medical professional who added the "Dracula" for a chilling sense of villainy? Perhaps this is a descendant of the first Dracula who recently acquired a medical license or some other doctoral degree.

Whatever the case, at least we can say for certain that his title doesn't make Doc Drac an inventor. Rather than create one, like a respectable mad scientist, Dr. Dracula *steals* the weapon he uses to terrorize America. "Hurray," cheers the weapon's inventor, Professor Fosdick, having dispatched a mouse from mortality with the *whoosh* of his new death ray. "It works, whoopee!"

A man so enthusiastic about a death ray seems to be asking for trouble, which is exactly what Fosdick gets when Dr. Dracula and his bat-winged assistants fly in the window. With long, drooling fangs jutting from under his bat-eared, emerald green cowl, Dr. Dracula inspires Fosdick to shout in terror, "Vampires! Vampires as large as men!" You have to wonder how large he thought vampires typically were. Dr. Dracula responds by turning the death ray on its inventor, reducing him instantly to a bare skeleton. "I will strike at America!" cries the German madman, adding the strangely worded coda, "I will sabotage her from end to end!"

These antics come to the attention of Captain Battle, a one-eyed tough guy in a star-spangled suit, and his kid sidekick, Hale (his full title is "Hale Battle," for the record). Via their all-seeing "Curvoscope," they witness Dr. Dracula's evil plans and jet off to combat him. The duo's jet-powered "Luciflyers" make the heroes an even match for the Doctor's winged assistants, although their terrifying appearance leads Hale to stammer: "Are they really v-v-vampires . . . ?"

Well, no, it turns out that they're not. "Just Nazi spies," declares Captain Battle, holding aloft a bat-winged suit, "who were very skillful in the art of gliding with artificial wings!" That doesn't explain their ominous fangs, but at least it clarifies why the vampires failed to exhibit transformation, increased strength, hypnosis, or the usual vampire errata. As a bonus, though, Hale gets to keep the wings for his souvenir shelf!

Enemy of: Captain Battle

Created by: Otto and Jack Binder

Debuted in: *Silver Streak Comics* #17 (Lev Gleason Publications, 1941)

Prescription: Take two death rays and call me in the morning.

DR. VOODOO

"Ah—what a mistake to think Dr. Voodoo can be eluded! What a mistake!"

Enemy of:
Brad Spencer, Wonder Man

Created by:
Bob Oksner and an uncredited writer

Debuted in:
Wonder Comics #9 (Better/Standard/Nedor, December 1946)

Question he's sick of answering:
Doctor *who* do?

THEY SAY YOU SHOULD dress for the job you want, not the job you have. If the intergalactic evildoer Dr. Voodoo is following that advice, it's difficult to say what job he's aiming for. In tuxedo and tails, he seems more prepared for a career as a maître d' or a cartoon mayor than the servant of an ever-living goddess of evil.

"Fearful as our earthly wars have been," begins the introductory caption to Dr. Voodoo's first appearance, "none can approach the carnage and destruction of the imminent invasion from the dark satellite of the moon where every evil soul that ever existed has taken refuge." A later caption celebrates Dr. V's accolades as well, claiming that no menace has ever been as threatening. After all, his lethal genius has "tapped the horrors of the universe!"

Dr. Voodoo emerges from the inky blackness of space in the company of Lilith, goddess of all evil, and her consort, the Immortal Emperor. While Dr. Voodoo's appearance is a little absurd—tux and tails, two clumps of hornlike hair on either side of his bald head, a Pan-like goatee—his look is downright staid compared to the Immortal Emperor. With a yellow, rhombus-shaped head split across the front by a cartoonish grin, the emperor appears to be an ecstatic novelty pencil eraser.

Still, the Emperor is married to the boss, and that means Voodoo must hop-to. Doubling down on the technobabble in his eternal war against Earth's defender Brad Spencer, aka Wonder Man, Voodoo unleashes squads of "anthrozoons" against "cosmoplanes" using "vapor guns," "frigitrons," and a "vacuum spiral," and later accepts assistance from a solar army of Thermodons.

For all his efforts, though, Dr. Voodoo doesn't seem too interested in capturing our embattled planet. "Is the world really worth conquering?" he ponders. "Its history isn't a pretty one. Wars . . . hatred . . ."

You'd imagine that wars and hatred would be right up the alley of a villain serving an evil goddess upon a planet of pure evil, but clearly Dr. Voodoo has refined tastes. When Lilith's planet—also called Lilith—is destroyed in a battle with Wonder Man, Dr. Voodoo searches for a new seat of the empire. But the queen of evil considers Earth her rightful domain. Harried and henpecked, Voodoo has no choice but to comply.

Dr. Voodoo and his allies disappeared from Wonder Man's ongoing narrative, though the hero's saga continued for a few more issues. Perhaps Voodoo was marshaling his anthrozoons when he should have been recharging his frigitrons for another attack on Earth's peaceful cosmoplanes.

WONDERMAN

Tally-HO
COMICS
10¢
GRRRRRRRR!!
SNOWMAN
The "SOMETHING NEW" in COMICS!
FOLLOW HIM AS HE TANGLES WITH THE MONSTER-MAKING
FANG!
ROAR!
John Giunta

FANG

"I, and my monsters, only remain! The world will soon be mine!"

SOMEWHERE IN THE DISTANT, shrouded oceans of the world is a terrible place haunted by a horrifying figure. "Desolation Island," describes the introductory caption. "It is an island of horror . . . only the faces of its inhabitants outdo the utter gloom of the scene . . ."

As wicked, fearsome, and unwanted as the fiends of Desolation Island may be, they live in dread of one of their fellow inhabitants. Possessed of a leering, skeletal maw resembling more the skull of an alligator than of a man, the hideous creature named Fang is feared more than anything, "even in our miserable world," mutters one of the island's disgruntled denizens.

So the cutthroats and crooks of Desolation Island tie Fang inside a sack and ferry him northward, to the frozen wastes far from their stomping grounds. In a classic count-your-chickens-before-they-hatch moment, the captain muses that they'll soon be free of Fang and the "imaginary but deadly" monsters he unleashes. He adds, "I'll take him so far . . . he'll never return! Swine!"

The captain leaves the bound Fang upon an ice floe to freeze to death, but Fang uses the jagged ice to cut himself free. Gesturing with his now-untied arms, Fang summons a sea serpent to drown the escaping vessel.

Fang sees that this arctic environment is populated by a peaceful native tribe and summons an army of monsters to subdue them. But when one soul prays hastily to a comical, cartoon snowman perched upon an elevated dais, the idol comes to life, *Frosty style*. The egg-headed, pink-cheeked rascal, who sports galoshes, cap, and a pipe, launches himself off his pedestal. "How long did this Fang character expect me to remain an idol?" he asks, adding, "I'll mow him down!"

The so-called Snowman makes short work of Fang's monster army, but superior numbers eventually see him captured. Face-to-face with the creature-summoning fiend, Snowman seems completely at his enemy's nonexistent mercy. Striking a gong that signals the opening of a trap door, Fang sends Snowman plummeting into a pit of "crocodiles." (They're clearly alligators, and also it's too cold for reptiles in the Arctic, but whatever!)

It's a strategy that quickly backfires. In no time at all, the plucky Snowman has thrown Fang into his very own alligator pit, where the merciless creatures tear him limb-from-limb. "The end of Fang!" Snowman declares. "But I'm going to stick around to make sure other Fangs don't show up!" The odds of that ever happening seem unlikely, but at least Snowman is there to keep his little coal eyes open.

VS

Enemy of:
Snowman

Created by:
John Giunta and Frank Frazetta

Debuted in:
Tally-Ho Comics #1 (Bailey Publishing, December 1944)

Favorite holiday:
Fangsgiving

THE HAWK

"Stand back, you fools! I'd soon kill you as argue!"

VS

Enemy of:
The Barker

Created by:
Klaus Nordling

Debuted in:
National Comics #55 (Quality Comics, August 1946)

Reason for turning to crime:
Building a nest egg

HOUGH STORIES IN THE Silver Age and onward often focus on villains' attempts to collect mystical arcana and conquer whole worlds, or even demolish the entire universe, the Golden Age baddies often worked small. A little kickback here and there seemed good enough, and protection rackets are a common motif.

This is the strategy employed by the bizarre Hawk, a thin-limbed, feather-coated weirdo who makes waves at the popular Colonel Lane Circus by scaring its performers right off the high wire. The success of the Wills Brothers, a trio of burly, carrot-topped acrobats, lures the Hawk into their dressing room. "At your service, gentlemen," he mutters menacingly while humbly bowing. "Always ready to give a stunt man a break—or a tumble—whichever he chooses!"

The frightened Wills Brothers are soon begging to be released from their contract. Revealing their problem to Carnie Calahan—secretly the Barker, a crime fighter whose beat was the carnival circuit—the eldest brother explains that the Hawk intends to extort every stuntman in the circus business. Recent accidental deaths of many big-top stuntmen at the hands—or talons—of an interfering bird of prey suggest that the would-be extortionist isn't bluffing.

The Hawk, as it turns out, enjoys a peculiar reputation: His enemies aren't sure if he's man or bird—or both! Undeterred, the Barker confronts the wretch and gives him the option of skipping town or getting hauled to the hoosegow.

The Hawk chooses neither, ducking behind a tree and emerging as a vicious, giant raptor who cleans up on the Barker and several of his sideshow assistants. Later, the same giant bird knocks one Wills brother from the high wire and threatens to startle a lion into chomping down on the head of his stand-in trainer—Carnie Calahan himself!

But as the lion grabs the hawk instead, the villain's duplicity is revealed. "Make that beast drop my bird!" shrieks the hidden, and very human, Hawk. Once the performers are sure that the Hawk is just a guy with a trained bird, they make short work of him. The circus's owner, Colonel Lane, recognizes the baddie as a former magician. "That accounts for his ability to pull disappearing acts and substitute himself for the bird," concludes the Barker.

In the end, everything works out all right for the circus. As the last performing Wills brother climbs into a cannon in preparation of being shot a hundred yards across the tent, he cheerfully confides in the Barker: "Boy, it's wonderful to feel safe and sound again!"

NATIONAL COMICS
THE BARKER
HERE THEY ARE, FOLKS... THE WORLD'S MOST DARING STUNT MEN, THE WILLS BROTHERS!
Even CARNIE CALAHAN, The Barker, becomes speechless when COLONEL LANE'S CIRCUS is turned into a mad melee by the dreaded HAWK!
50¢
By Klaus Nordling

THE HORRIBLE HAND

[rude gesture]

VS

Enemy of:
Ibis the Invincible

Created by:
Bob Hebberd and an uncredited writer

Debuted in:
Whiz Comics #34 (Fawcett Comics, September 1942)

How it's defeated:
Handily

SOMETIMES EVIL IS SO inherent within a villain that not even an entire body is required for evil-doing. In at least one case, all a terrible force for wickedness needed was a disembodied hand. Detached body parts are a fairly frequent staple of comic book baddies. On several occasions, Superman, Supergirl, Aquaman, and Batman—just to name a few—have all fought giant, independent hands, feet, eyes, and even mouths.

The villainous wizard Trug was a frequent foe of Ibis the Invincible, an ancient Egyptian wizard who awoke in the modern day after 4,000 years of uninterrupted sleep in his tomb. Dedicated to battling evil with the power of his almost omnipotent "Ibistick"—"It performs miracles of white magic," explains Ibis—the ancient magician at one point destroys Trug's sorcerous skills.

Seeking an alternative means of mayhem, Trug visits the stately home of Crowley Thorne, a black market broker for sinister sorcerers. There, Trug finds himself in the possession of a disembodied, floating, and malevolent red hand trapped within a modest metal bird cage. Crowley describes the massive mitt as "the hand of a devil," capable of receiving and obeying commands.

What can a demon hand do for a malevolent menace like Trug? Steal great treasures? Strangle his enemies? Scratch his back? Well, he gives the first two a try, sending the hand to rob the "State Bank" and then, in a complicated follow-up, frame Ibis for the murder of a police sergeant.

While Ibis is busy extricating himself from jail, his partner Taia is vulnerable to Trug's desire for revenge. Commanding the hand to throttle Taia dead, the wicked wizard is interrupted by Ibis's timely intervention. "Ibistick," he commands his powerful weapon, "send flames to scorch that devil thing!" The hotfoot (well, hothand) sends the devil hand scuttling. After encasing the five-fingered fink in a globe of impenetrable crystal, Ibis finds capturing Trug to be a simple matter.

Later, Ibis disposes of the hand, although not by the most secure method. "I'll bury this Hand of Horror and hide all traces," he explains as he digs into the dirt, adding, "Let mother earth keep the secret forever!" That's a good solution, until a hungry dog comes along and digs it up, but perhaps it's sufficient for now.

IBIS
The Invincible
HE HAS COME, SPANNING 4000 YEARS OF TIME, TO FACE AND FIGHT THE EVILS THAT BESET US IN THE TWENTIETH CENTURY....
THOUGH FORCES OF FANTASTIC POWER CONFRONT HIM, IBIS, the Invincible, WIELDS AGAINST THEM THE MIGHT OF THE IBISTICK, WAND OF WHITE MAGIC, GIVEN TO HIM TO USE FOR THE GOOD OF MANKIND! BUT BLACK MAGIC ALMOST OVERCAME WHITE IN THE ADVENTURE OF
"The HORRIBLE HAND!"

TRUG, THE WICKED WIZARD, IS MAKING A STRANGE CALL....
WHAT DO YOU WANT?
ARE YOU CROWLEY THORNE? MY NAME IS TRUG, AND...

I'M MR. THORNE'S SERVANT! HE'S EXPECTING YOU! COME IN!

THE WIZARD
WITH ROY, THE SUPER-BOY
by Paul Reinman
Death will come to every man
Nor asking if it can-
And the trail it leaves behind
mortal man will never find
NIGHT- AND THROUGH THE FOG THAT GIRDS THE TOWERS OF MAN-HATTAN COMES A SCREAM OF TERROR AND OF DEATH!.. THE JINGLER HAS STRUCK AGAIN, AND A WHOLE CITY TREMBLES-FEAR-FUL OF THE MAD POET WHO WRITES HIS VERSES IN THE RED INK OF BLOOD. HERE IS, INDEED, A SIN-ISTER OPPONENT FOR THE WIZARD AND ROY THE SUPER-BOY..."THE JINGLER OF DEATH."
OUT OF THE MURKY DARKNESS A BODY HURTLES EARTHWARD-
THERE HE IS-SEND FOR AN AM-BULANCE!
HE'S DEAD! EVERY BONE IN HIS BODY IS BROKEN-AND THIS POEM IN HIS HAND...THIS LOOKS LIKE MORE OF THE JINGLER'S WORK!
1

THE JINGLER

"Poetry—and death! What a rare combination!"

OMIC BOOKS ARE FILLED with deranged and evil types from any variety of professions: mad scientists and doctors, soulless tyrants, amoral actors, and even a surprising number of terrifying toymakers (the Murder Marionettes, for example). However, occupying a tiny niche of criminal craftsmanship is the *evil poet*.

The Jingler (aka "the Jingler of Death") begins his career not as an evil poet, but merely as a pretty bad one. Edward Fearing, "a poverty-stricken poet" (redundancy alert), unsuccessfully peddles his rhymes around town, only to have the door repeatedly slammed in his face. "If that's poetry, I'll eat it," proclaims one cruel book publisher.

The destitute poet is caught stealing by a shopkeeper, and accidentally kills the man. Dashing off in a panic, he neglects to notice that his victim clutches one of Fearing's poems in his lifeless grip.

But the newspapers *do* notice. The next morning, the front page bears Fearing's doggerel in a story about the crime: "Once I wrote a little rhyme / Of people in an older time." Not exactly Robert Frost, but it sells papers.

"So they said my verses would never be published," Fearing crows in his candlelit apartment. "I had to murder to get my verses read—but it's worth it! If it's murder they want, they'll have it," he adds, following a train of thought that's probably crossed the mind of every unpublished writer at some point.

Dubbed "The Jingler" by the papers, Fearing attacks assorted publishing moguls as revenge for their constant snubbing. In one particularly gruesome killing, he stuffs a poetry-laden piece of paper down the throat of the publisher who earlier offered to eat Fearing's words. That'll show him!

The Jingler's high-profile crimes draw the attention of the Wizard and his kid sidekick, Roy the Super-Boy. Sporting a highly trained "Super-Brain," the Wizard deduces that all the victims worked in the publishing industry. Some deduction! It's enough of a lead, however, that the Wizard and Roy are able to determine the Jingler's next target—a renowned literary critic preparing to judge the Jingler's death poems live and on air!

The confrontation between the Jingler and the Wizard leads from the studio to a high cliff face, down which both men tumble as they battle. The Wizard lands safely, but the Jingler is dashed against the rocks. In an ironic twist, one of his poems flutters downward and lands upon the now-still chest of the larcenous lyricist. The Jingler's final words: "Life quickly cools / in poets and fools / One more life, my friend / is approaching its end."

VS

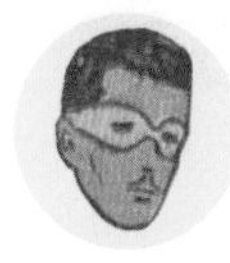

Enemy of:
The Wizard and Roy the Super-Boy

Created by:
Bill Woolfolk and Paul Reinman

Debuted in:
Top-Notch Comics #26 (MLJ Comics, April 1942)

Weapons of choice:
Homicidal haiku; sinister sonnets; limericks

KING KILLER

"Why did I do that? I never kicked dogs before . . . but now I like to kill!!!"

Enemy of:
Uncle Sam

Created by:
Will Eisner

Debuted in:
Uncle Sam Quarterly #1 (Quality Comics, Autumn 1941)

Line of succession:
Prince Pickpocket, Princess Purse-Snatcher, Baron Burglary, Earl of Parking in a Handicap Spot

SOME CRIMINALS ARE BORN to great villainy; others have great villainy thrust upon them. The latter is true of the nameless figure who eventually becomes King Killer, the King of Crime.

Two names we do know, however, are those of Dr. Link and Dr. Blink. Egg-headed mad scientists, the identical doctors hatch a bizarre and dangerous scheme. Collecting the cadavers of recently deceased notorious criminals, they set in motion a plan to create an "arch-fiend" and "super-criminal" whose unstoppable powers for evil will make them rich with ill-gotten gains.

The sinister surgeons pack the slim frame of their test subject—a 98-pound weakling from the streets—with the brains of some of the underworld's most infamous killers, thieves, hit men, and gangland chiefs. A hearty transfusion of gorilla blood completes the operation. In the place of the once-slight figure rises King Killer, seven-feet of muscle and murder. His teeth have grown into fangs, his clothing is stretched and torn over his new-found superhuman muscles, and a terrible scar runs across the middle of his skull—a reminder of the criminal brains that now drive his body.

King Killer lives up to his name (both parts of it, in fact). In short order, he murders the bully who once tormented him, slays a shopkeeper for the contents of his safe, and even snuffs out Doctors Blink and Link when they exhibit the audacity to ask for a cut of the ill-gotten gains. "By thunder," he bellows in triumph, "from now on, I take what I want!!!"

What Killer apparently wants is to indulge his kingly side with uncontested power over a sovereign state in the Republic. He brings almost every criminal in the United States together in the middle of the open desert, where they build their own city—of crime! Before long, Congress is voting to admit the new state of Rex to the Union, unaware that they're granting King Killer his fondest wish. "We shall be the haven of every criminal in the country," he boasts, adding, "A kingdom of crime in the heart of America!! And I am the King!!!" A veritable army of crooks is more than happy to take up residence in his domain. Committing crimes in nearby Everytown, they race back across the border to Rex, eluding pursuing police once they cross the state line.

These antics eventually bring Rex and its royalty to the attention of Uncle Sam, the apotheosis of the patriotic hero motif. While other star-spangled superheroes like Captain America and the Shield draped themselves in flag-like costumes, Uncle Sam was the real deal . . . not just a guy dressed like the famous →

Chapter 2.

UNCLE SAM

William Eisner

I WANT YOU poster, mind you, but the *actual* Uncle Sam. Tracing his origins back to the days of the American Revolution, Uncle Sam used his powers to fight for America in every battle from Valley Forge to Normandy Beach. Obviously, a rogue American state is just the kind of thing to get his red-white-and-blue blood boiling.

Soon an epic battle is undertaken on the fields of Rex, as Uncle Sam and King Killer put their equally titanic strength to the test. The clash lays waste to the entirety of the recently created state. Uncle Sam prevails, and the would-be tyrant is imprisoned in his own dungeon. Of course, in later issues King Killer makes his escape to further bedevil Uncle Sam. He even invites Hitler and Mussolini to visit his new kingdom of crime! Luckily, Uncle Sam is there to put an end to that scheme as well.

EDITOR'S NOTE...

Both King Killer and Uncle Sam were the products of Will Eisner, one of comicdom's most prolific and influential creators. His most famous character, the Spirit, faced off against an array of unusual foes, including the actor-turned-villain Mister Midnight, the buzzard-loving Mister Carrion, and the mostly unseen master of crime known as the Octopus.

AS THE ARMORED MONSTER BEARS DOWN UPON HIM, UNCLE SAM LEAPS ASIDE AND SWINGS...
COME OUT OF THAT CHEESE-BOX YOU RAT!!!
AAAAAAAAA
COMB THIS OUTA YER BEARD FANCY PANTS!
CRASH!
?
HERE I AM!
..AND HERE YOU GO!
ZIP
THE SUN SETS AND RISES, AND STILL THE WARRIORS CONTINUE THEIR TITANIC STRUGGLE, CLEAVING A PATH OF DESTRUCTION THROUGH THE CITY WITH THEIR THRASHING FISTS...
ZOOM
?

PLANET COMICS PAGE 21

Buzz Crandall of the Space Patrol

By Bob Jordan.

BUZZ CRANDALL LIVES ON THE HIGHLY CIVILIZED PLANET OF VENUS, AND IS IN CHARGE OF THE INTER-PLANETARY SECRET SERVICE FOR BOTH VENUS AND THE EARTH. HE HAS BECOME THE TOP CRIME-BUSTER OF THE UNIVERSE . . . .

LEPUS THE FIEND

"I shall destroy all the civilized planets!"

VS

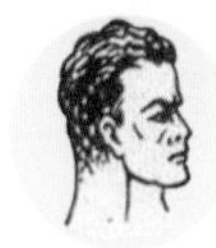

Enemy of:
Buzz Crandall

Created by:
Fletcher Hanks
(as "Bob Jordan")

Debuted in:
Planet Comics #7
(Fiction House,
July 1940)

Fun fact:
Lepus is Latin for "rabbit"

FLETCHER HANKS IS A legendary comics creator best known for his bizarre, dreamlike tales and distinctive outsider art. He is most famous for nearly omnipotent superheroes like skull-faced jungle goddess Fantomah and Stardust the Super-Wizard. But even his mere mortals exhibit his peculiar approach to storytelling. When his heroes aren't wielding limitless powers and executing colorful punishments, you can count on his villains to do it for them.

Such is the case of Lepus "the fiend," a fur-covered misanthrope who seeks to destroy the entire universe. He makes plenty of trouble for Buzz Crandall of the Space Patrol, who detects strange, powerful rays being used against the planet Venus. Subjected to tremendous forces, the world is torn out of its orbit. Meanwhile Crandall's assistant on Earth, Sandra Hale, warns him of similar danger on that world. Hey, that's our planet!

The culprit is Lepus—the sneering, shirtless, hair-slathered menace who is operating from the confines of a nearby blazing star. "I shall make all the universe wild and primitive," he declares. First on his agenda: making Earth and Venus crash into each other.

But Buzz Crandall has a plan, too. Rocketing towards the source of the mysterious rays in his "ray-proof cruiser" (good thinking, Buzz!), he prepares his own super-powerful weapon: a rapid-fire interplanetary gun that will "demolish his outfit!" Buzz and Sandra battle their way towards Lepus's planet-smashing machine even as the evil creature's rays are wreaking genuine havoc. "On the Earth, the temperature all over the globe has become below zero, and the days and nights last only a few minutes," explains a caption in a panel depicting a crowd of desperate people taking to the woods. Their dash for safety serves little purpose, unfortunately. A grim caption explains, "People perish by the thousands as the two planets leave their orbits."

The wild Lepus has a ferocious hatred for civilization, but he doesn't have very good math skills. A miscalculation on his part causes Venus and Earth to narrowly avoid striking one another. Before he can recalculate, Crandall's opposing ray gun does its work. Lepus's scientific stronghold crumbles, and the planets slide back into their regular orbits without any further struggle or disaster. As for Lepus, he suffers the justice delivered upon all intergalactic villains who seek to smash planets for fun—he is killed off-panel, his corpse showing up after the fact on a celebratory Crandall's all-seeing view screen.

MR. NIGHT

"Go away puny Earthling! These men are under the protection of Mr. Night!"

Enemy of:
Mary Marvel

Created by:
Otto and Jack Binder

Debuted in:
Wow Comics #14 (Fawcett Comics, June 1943)

Hex code:
#000000

SUPERVILLAINS COME IN ALL shapes and sizes, based on all sorts of themes. And they dress in all sorts of colors . . . but only one is a living, abstract *idea* of color. More specifically, an incarnation of the absence of color. That bizarre distinction belongs to Mr. Night!

The premise—evil embodiment of absolute blackness who threatens a magical kingdom of color so as to drench the world in darkness and rule it forever—seems like something straight out of a fairy tale. Especially since the entire adventure begins with a crook chasing a rainbow in a quest to steal a pot of gold!

All of this takes place in the world of Mary Marvel, a member of the Marvel Family clan and a character whose adventures often had the whimsical logic and seeming free-association of children's bedtime stories. Teaming up with child prodigy Creighton Tinkerman, Mary investigates the youngster's discovery of a genuine pot of gold at the end of the rainbow. Gold that the crooked gangster Porky Snork and his men are also hotly pursuing.

A fight upon a hijacked hot-air balloon sees all the players in the drama dropped off in the Color Kingdom of Rainbow City, "Arbor of the Sky Spirits," according to a shibboleth above the city gates. Meeting with King Color, Mary receives a quick education in the importance of the seemingly mythical realm. This is the place where all colors come from. "The colors of dawn and sunset, of autumn, of the Aurora Borealis, of pictures," explains the rainbow regent, thankfully abbreviating his list. Then he warns Mary of the insidious Mr. Night, an evil sky spirit banished from the city and deadly enemy of the King.

Indeed Mr. Night, with the aid of Porky Snork and his men, is already enacting his color-killing plan. He invades the Color Factory of Jack Frost (where the colors of the seasons are mixed) and abducts the King's daughter Aurora, the spirit of dawn. He plans to hold her for ransom . . . namely, all the color in Rainbow City! Which he will then destroy, turning the whole world jet black. "And I'll rule the Earth! Ha Ha!"

He seems to make a bit of a leap, but it's a moot point. Mary Marvel zooms to "the gloomy reaches of Nightland" With a single punch, she knocks the fiend through the bricks of his own castle. Unfortunately, doing so allows him to escape. "Slipped away in the dark," Mary *tsk*s, "I shouldn't have hit him so hard!"

Still, like all good fairy tales, the princess is saved, the bad guy is defeated, and everyone in the Kingdom of Color lives happily ever after. The end.

WOW COMICS

A FAWCETT MAGAZINE

10¢

JUNE
NO. 14

MARY MARVEL
FIGHTS MR. NIGHT
FOR THE
POT OF GOLD!

68 PAGES IN FULL COLOR

42
AMERICA'S GREATEST COMICS
MINUTE-MAN
The ONE MAN ARMY
meets MR. SKELETON!
"MINUTE MAN"-DONT ATTEMPT TO RESCUE US-ITS TOO TERRIBLE! EVEN NOW DEATH IS STARING AT US"- THESE WORDS CAME OVER THE PHONE, SENDING THE ONE MAN ARMY ON A NEVER-TO BE-FORGOTTEN TRAIL OF A RUTHLESS MURDERER! A KILLER KNOWN AS MR. SKELETON.. WHO CHALLENGES MINUTE-MAN TO A DUEL OF DEATH!
AT A SECLUDED SPOT IN THE COUNTRY... AND THE PRESIDENT OF THE UNITED STATES GATHERS WITH SOME DIPLOMATS FOR A SECRET CONFERENCE.
SOMEONE'S TRYING TO MURDER THE PRESIDENT!
A RIFLE SHOT!

MR. SKELETON

"Take a look, stupid generals! This is what I have in store for all of you! The skeleton bath! Ha ha ha!"

SOME SUPERVILLAINS HAVE TO put in years of work to establish their particular brand of lawlessness. But some supervillains have it easier . . . some are fifteen feet tall and so famous that their handiwork is evident even when they don't introduce themselves.

Such is the case with Mr. Skeleton, a desiccated fiend who looms over his heroic foe and has a yen for boiling the flesh from his captives. When he first encounters the patriotic pugilist Minute-Man, it's following an attempt on the life of the president of the United States. While the hero pursues the gunman, Mr. Skeleton and his agents abduct several of the top U.S. brass assembled for a diplomatic conference—including Minute-Man's friend and mentor, General Milton.

"Minute-Man, don't try to save us," pleads the desperate voice of the kidnapped General during a hasty phone call. "Death will be your penalty—it is too late to help! G- G- Goodbye!" The warning has the opposite effect, as the One Man Army pledges to his missing chief: "They've got you, but remember one thing—Minute-Man will meet Mister Skeleton!"

This is an impressive trick on Minute-Man's part, seeing as how no one had mentioned Mr. Skeleton before this point. Still, his instincts are spot-on; the aforementioned baddie is indeed responsible for the abductions. He threatens the captured Generals with a dip in what Mr. Skeleton calls his "skeleton bath"—a boiling cauldron of flesh-eating liquid which reduces living beings to stripped bone in a matter of seconds!

Minute-Man saves Milton from the towering, whisper-thin monstrosity, but fails to save the other two Generals, or to prevent Mr. Skeleton from abducting even more of them. "You both have the brains to lead an army," the giant tells his new captives, "An army against the United States! If you'll come over to my side—I'll spare your lives!"

Naturally, the freedom-loving captives instruct Mr. Skeleton to go jump in a lake, and Minute-Man rejoins the battle—aided by a fully-armed American platoon. The fiend exhibits the full extent of his power in this battle, shrugging off bullets and smashing heavy artillery like toys. He doesn't account for Minute-Man's martial prowess, however, and for his trouble ends up smashed against a wall—shattered into a thousand pieces, reduced instantly to a pile of smoking bones! All his power and reputation coming to naught. It's an ignoble end for a villain so evil that heroes apparently knew his name without ever having heard it before.

Enemy of:
Minute-Man (the One Man Army)

Created by:
Phil Bard and an uncredited writer

Debuted in:
America's Greatest Comics #1 (Fawcett Comics, September 1941)

College fraternity:
Skull and Bones

REEFER KING

"Scoop up those reefers and makins. You gotta help me harvest the crop before we scram!"

VS

Enemy of:
Yankee Boy

Created by:
Sam Cooper

Debuted in:
Dynamic Comics #16 (Harry "A" Chesler, October 1945)

Not to be confused with:
Burger King (though he often hangs out in the parking lot there)

EVERY FORM OF AMERICAN media has, at one point or another, addressed the perceived threat of marijuana use by engaging in some elaborate hyperbole. Healthy, vibrant youngsters are turned into leering, hunched-over maniacs. Scintillating intellects are draped in never-ending psychosis. Law-abiding citizens become hardened, murder-happy gunslingers overnight, all in the name of feeding a ravenous habit. Reefer madness!

One Mary Jane–laced menace is the so-called Reefer King, a shady dealer of "funny cigarettes." (At no point in this story are the illicit cigarettes ever referred to as marijuana or cannabis.) Taking advantage of a wartime shortage of tobacco products, King—aided by the equally violent Kreeper—approaches shopkeepers with an alluring offer. "At a dime per cig," he tells the humble owner of an otherwise legit cigar store, "you'll be makin' yourself a hunnert percent profit, Mac. An' when your customers get in the habit, you'll be in clover!"

It's too good an offer to pass up, which is how Mac ends up selling "somethin' new" to innocent teenage tobacco aficionado Mickey. There's certainly something jarring—even amusingly ironic—about a story that condemns the use of marijuana while blithely approving of the unhealthy habit of underage smoking.

Puffing away in a filthy back alley, the Reefer King's insidious cigarettes effect a strange change on the youngster. He notes that the smoke makes him "think different." Producing a toy pistol from nowhere, Mickey tells us: "This four-bit cap pistol looks like a real gun in the dark. I'M GETTIN' IDEAS!" Mickey's joint-inspired attempt to hold up a gas station gets him slapped around by an attendant and hauled off to prison.

Soon local law enforcement informs all-American teen Vic Martin, aka Yankee Boy, about the "bad cigarettes" being sold around town. When Yankee Boy confronts King, the kahuna of cannabis is quick to turn to violence, pulling a gun on Yankee Boy and firing wildly into the streets. For good measure he shoots Mac, the cigar shop owner, directly in the face.

Yankee Boy pursues King back to his hideout, where he engages in a knock-down, dragout battle with King and Kreeper. The duo attack Yankee Boy with clubs and scythes, but in the end they're defeated by the kid hero. Forced to walk back to police headquarters, the King and his partner reflect on the ultimate lesson of their wickedness: "Why wuz we so dumb, King?" asks Kreeper.

ON THE LOOKOUT, HAPPY!
MUCH TIME READING ABOUT THE CRIME WAVE?
YANKEE BOY
SORRY—NO CIGARETTES TODAY!
But in spite of this sign, the clerk knows people will whisper "I'll wait till the others go out, then you'll slip me a pack, huh?" These under handed sales were made-to-order for The Reefer King -- a sinister salesman of cigarettes that shrivel the smokers' souls! How could Yankee Boy -- alone and unaided -- dethrone the devil behind this crooked commerce?
Late one evening at the cigar store on the corner of Main and Elm Streets in Yankee Boy's home town--
YOU WON'T HAVE NO TROUBLE WITH TH' COPS, MAC, IF YOU SELL 'EM ONLY TO YOUR REG'LAR CUSTOMERS!
OKAY, I'LL TAKE THE CHANCE, MISTER!
AT A DIME PER CIG, YOU'LL BE MAKIN' YOURSELF A HUNNERT PERCENT PROFIT, MAC AN' WHEN YOUR CUSTOMERS GET IN THE HABIT, YOU'LL BE IN CLOVER!
Later that night---
NO CIGS, EH, MAC?
MAYBE YOU'D LIKE TO TRY SOMETHIN' NEW, MICKEY! A DIME APIECE!

100 PAGE POCKET COMICS

POCKET COMICS

No. 2

SEPT. 10¢

PDC

CONTINUE THE ADVENTURES OF THE GREAT NEW STARS!

★ SPIRIT OF '76 BATTLES SATAN

★ THE BLACK CAT ★ RED BLAZER

★ THE ZEBRA .... and many others

SATAN

"Foiled again! Oh . . . why can't I die?"

"SATAN," PROCLAIMS HIS INTRODUCTION, "mad dictator of the underworld! Wherever there is crime, brutality, death in the world, there is Satan!"

So it seems! From his infernal throne in a chamber filled with hidden deathtraps, Satan commands a nationwide network of spies and saboteurs, pausing only to drop one of them through a trap door to a spike-filled floor below or to take an urgent phone call from Hitler. Then he organizes high-octane acts of evil to undo America's military efforts. Adding insult to injury, he uses the Statue of Liberty's torch to send messages to hidden Nazi subs, resulting in a terrible battle which sinks the fleet in New York's harbor. Fond of machine guns, he slays dozens of factory workers and ends the lives of important bigwigs at a fancy opera house. Whatever else you can say about him, evidently Satan doesn't discriminate across economic classes.

The red-skinned demonic figure's primary goal on earth: find some means by which he can be permanently rendered dead!

Notwithstanding his satanic visage, Satan only shares his appearance and name with his Biblical forebear. In fact, 500 years earlier, he had been an unnamed Spanish explorer seeking the Fountain of Youth. Evidently having found the Fountain of Turning into a Horrible Devil Man instead, he's transformed on the spot. Adding to his shock and despair is the discovery that he apparently cannot die. Satan takes the worst that a handful of superheroes (including Air Cadet Jim Brady, Agent 99, and the patriotic Spirit of '76), has to offer. He gets poisoned by his own tarantula, and willingly jumps from a plane. Ultimately, he walks away unscathed.

The closest Satan comes to permanent death involves a lemon-yellow doppelganger named Natas, who takes umbrage at Satan's claim of being the "Lord of Evil." To prove which one of them is actually the most evil creature on Earth, the pair sign an agreement: "Know you all men of evil . . . on this day Satan and Natas agree that whosoever does most wrong shall rightfully be Lord of Evil." That cannot be a binding legal document. Their contest ends when the two turn machine guns on one another as if choreographed. "When the smoke clears," explains the caption, "their blasted bodies wallow helplessly in a widening pool of blood."

Satan collapses, seemingly—and finally—dead. Or, at the very least, cancelled, as Pocket Comics ended publication after its fourth issue, and Satan failed to reappear in any of the line's other titles. Perhaps he got his wish.

VS

Enemy of:
Spirit of '76, Agent 99, Natas, and more

Created by:
Otto Binder and Pierce Rice

Debuted in:
Pocket Comics #1 (Harvey Comics, August 1941)

Not to be confused with:
Satanas (see next page)

SATANAS

"At last ... the vault! Soon all the gold in America will be mine!"

VS

Enemy of:
The Bogeyman

Created by:
Sam Cooper and an uncredited writer

Debuted in:
Red Band Comics #1 (Rural Home, November 1944)

Not to be confused with:
Satan (see previous page)

THERE MUST BE SOME small component of supervillainy which is predicated on living up to one's reputation. But the threat of evil can be such a profound source of fear and dread that some scoundrels end up being less menacing than the claims of their press release.

Take, for example, the opening caption which introduces Satanas, a cyclopean, green-skinned fashion plate from Pluto, as "The most evil man in the universe." The hype continues: "From out of the frightful depths of intergalactic space comes the most foul plague our world has ever known! Satanas . . . cynical, sneering, too evil for his own kind—comes to conquer our world!"

The authorities on Satanas's native Pluto do little to mitigate his rep. Prior to sentencing him to eternal exile, the magistrate indulges a hideous hagiography of the green meanie. "We of Pluto are not a kindly race," he explains. "We make no pretense of honor, we have no particular virtues, but *you*, Satanas, have gone too far! You make vice a virtue . . . cruelty a practice . . ."

Immortal and indestructible, Satanas spends centuries in space, plotting for his moment of opportunity once the ship's atomic motor gives out. When it does, he finds Pluto impossible to locate but, being within spitting distance of Earth, he decides to make the best of a bad situation and conquer humanity instead. "This is your master," he announces over a hijacked radio broadcast. "I shall conquer the world! In order to do that, I shall need money!"

Armed with a paralysis ray and disintegrator gun, Satanas launches an assault on Fort Knox, making off with—according to the numbers helpfully written on the side of the sacks he's purloined—about ten billion dollars in easy-to-carry gold. The assembled federal men and armed forces laugh off the theft, possibly misunderstanding international economics. "I'm laughing because I'm picturing Satanas's face when he finds out America has been off the gold standard for years," chuckles one G-man. A tank gunner replies, "He won't be able to spend it here in the United States! All that work for nothing!"

Never really living up to his press, Satanas spends most of his crooked career facing off against Red Band Comics's domino-masked do-gooder the Bogeyman—on covers, anyway. Despite gracing the fronts of many comics, he only appeared in one interior tale. Perhaps it was the underwhelming evil of his debut crime, or perhaps he was too busy gleefully spending his billions, but Satanas's reign of terror stops short after a single adventure.

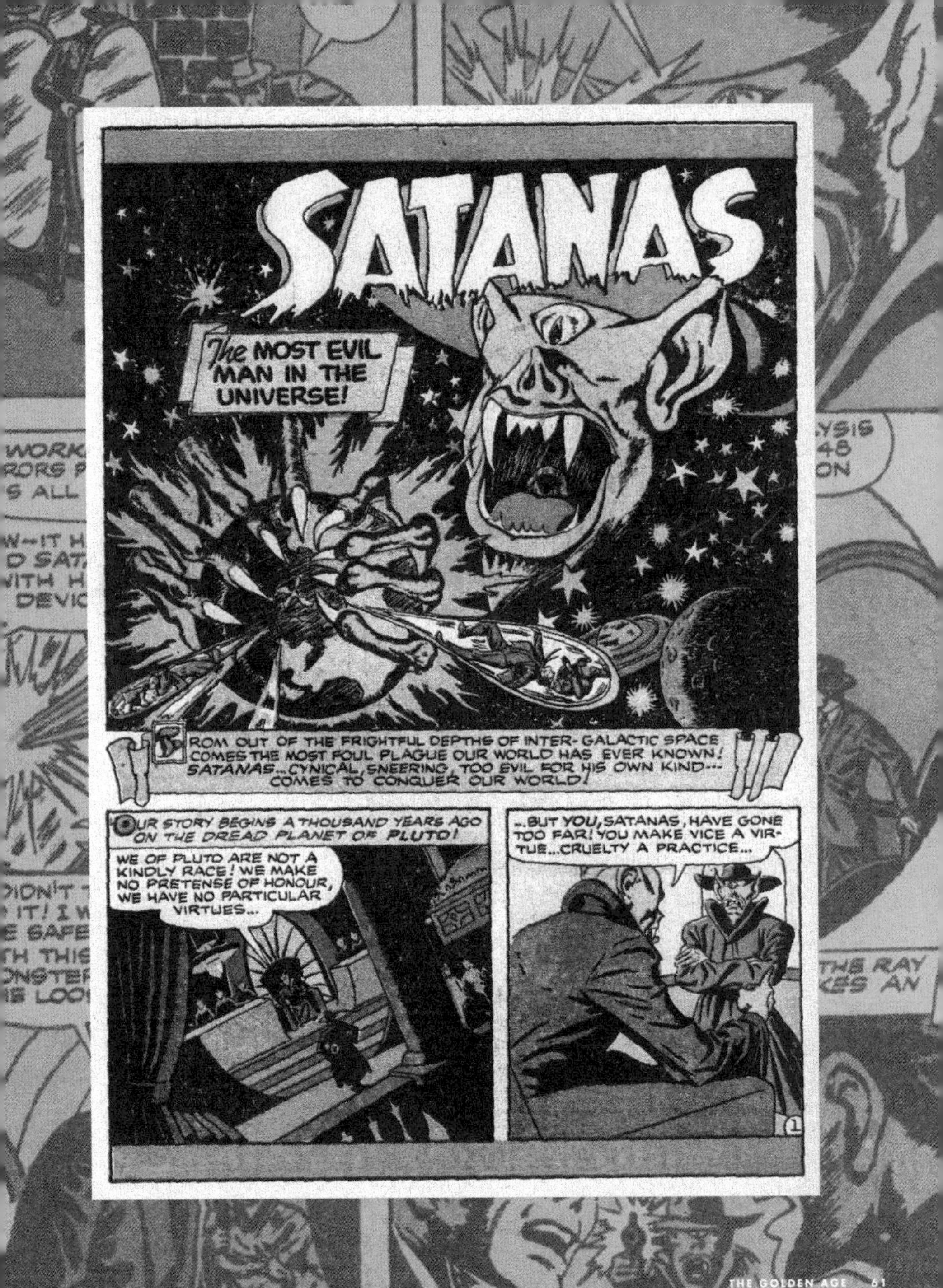

SATANAS

The MOST EVIL MAN IN THE UNIVERSE!

FROM OUT OF THE FRIGHTFUL DEPTHS OF INTER-GALACTIC SPACE COMES THE MOST FOUL PLAGUE OUR WORLD HAS EVER KNOWN! SATANAS...CYNICAL, SNEERING, TOO EVIL FOR HIS OWN KIND--- COMES TO CONQUER OUR WORLD!

SO, YOU'VE COME TO INVESTIGATE US ?

SEAWEED QUEEN

"Look in there if you want to see what will become of you!"

HE SEA CONTAINS MANY mysteries, and even more menace. Besides rough seas, storms, tsunamis, terrifying predators, and the practically quotidian threat of drowning in the deep ocean, there are also unnamable dangers. For instance, seaweed people and their chlorophyll-sucking whirlpool of death!

Ships and subs are disappearing in a specific patch of gulf water, and sailor and hardy investigator Kinks Mason volunteers to check it out. But he's soon pulled underwater by writhing strands of seaweed, seemingly driven by a malevolent intelligence.

The master of the seaweed is, appropriately enough, the Seaweed Queen, who commands an army of horrifying Seaweed Monsters. As if to underline the inequities of the class system, while all the seaweed people possess lower bodies made of grimy, swirling masses of seaweed, only the Queen has been gifted with a lovely, human face and upper body. Her subjects have faces like chronically ill brussels sprouts, or wax cabbages left to rest under a heat lamp.

With Kinks slated to suffer the same fate as the other humans collected from the previously captured vessels, the Seaweed Queen reveals "our chlorophyll manufacturing plant," indicating a titanic machine which violently churns the water above their heads. "The great whirlpool captures and magnifies the rays of the sun," she explains. "We convert the vital element into the making of chlorophyll. The clinging weed which pulled your ship under the sea has been vitalized by it!"

The Seaweed People need the chlorophyll to live—and to turn human beings into seaweed-monster slaves! Chlorophyll really has a thousand uses. It's like the baking soda of the ocean floor.

Now fully informed of the Seaweed Kingdom's horrible plan, Kinks starts a fight with the Seaweed Monsters (many of whom are human beings who were transformed by multipurpose chlorophyll). Then he dashes off to a nearby submarine, launches a torpedo into the manufacturing plant, and doubles down by dynamiting the nearby store of chlorophyll.

Deprived of their life-giving substance, the Seaweed Creatures—and their Queen—perish suddenly and quietly in midpursuit of the escaping Mason, dropping dead where they stand (or float, or swim—this all takes place underwater). For his part, Kinks gets a medal, which isn't too bad for snuffing an entire race of world-conquering sea-beasts.

VS

Enemy of:
Kinks Mason

Created by:
Steve Broder

Debuted in:
Captain Flight #5 (Fiction House, December 1944)

Sung to the tune of:
"Dancing Queen" by ABBA

SPLINTER

"This breaks our contract and your neck!"

Enemy of:
Granny Gumshoe

Created by:
Gill Fox

Debuted in:
National Comics #57 (Quality Comics, December 1946)

Weaknesses:
Wood rot; Dutch elm disease; termites

ORLD-FAMOUS VENTRILOQUIST Professor Hiram Echo is nearly apoplectic with worry. In his dressing room, staring at his dummy Splinter, he mutters fearfully to himself. "Unbelievable!! I've used that dummy so long that I've come to regard it as human!" With genuine dread, he voices his deepest fear: "I think I've caused a spark of life to burn in its wooden bosom!!"

Continuing to elucidate his concern, the Professor concludes that during a performance that very afternoon, the dummy actually spoke to him, saying "Tonight, revenge!" Furthermore, he has a premonition that "Something against the laws of nature will happen . . . the dummy will come to life!!"

Professor Echo was genuinely prescient, for no sooner does that evening's show begin than Splinter abdicates his position on Echo's knee and storms off the stage. "Tonight I quit!" he says of his own volition. "I'll settle with you in the dressing room!"

While no explanation is given for Splinter's sudden animation, his grim promise is very real. Splinter slugs Echo with a deadly blow, killing his former master instantly. Witness to this is Granny Gumshoe, an elderly and only-seemingly frail old woman who solves unusual and mysterious crimes in her spare time. Granny follows Splinter to his next appointment, with a dummy manufacturer. There, like the Frankenstein Monster demanded of his creator, Splinter demands the creation of "a beautiful girl dummy" to be his partner.

The incredulous dummy maker is about to get his head bashed in when Granny arrives to stop a second murder. "I invent the queerest things," she says, loading rubber cement into a spray gun which she had built into her umbrella. Splinter escapes the sticky assault, but Granny is hot on his tail. The deadly dummy also shrugs off a bullet through the middle of his forehead, patching it with wood filler, but panics at the sight of Granny's beaker full of termites! Chasing Splinter to the hickory tree from which he was originally carved, Granny ends his reign of terror by chopping it down—killing both tree and dummy with one stroke.

The murders may have been ended, but Splinter's story still ends on a gruesome note. Granny uses Splinter's head and torso as the base for a decorative living room lamp!

NATIONAL COMICS
GRANNY GUMSHOE
GRANNY!
SOMEWHERE IN THE SUBURBS OF WESTON LIVES A LOVABLE, OLD LADY! NO ONE WOULD HAVE BELIEVED THAT THIS QUAINT PERSON HAD A SECRET PASSION FOR CRIMINAL INVESTIGATION AND INVENTION.. THESE HOBBIES CAME IN HANDY WHEN GRANNY GUMSHOE GOT INVOLVED IN A STRANGE ADVENTURE! IT ALL STARTED WHEN HER GRANDDAUGHTER, LIPPY LU, CALLED

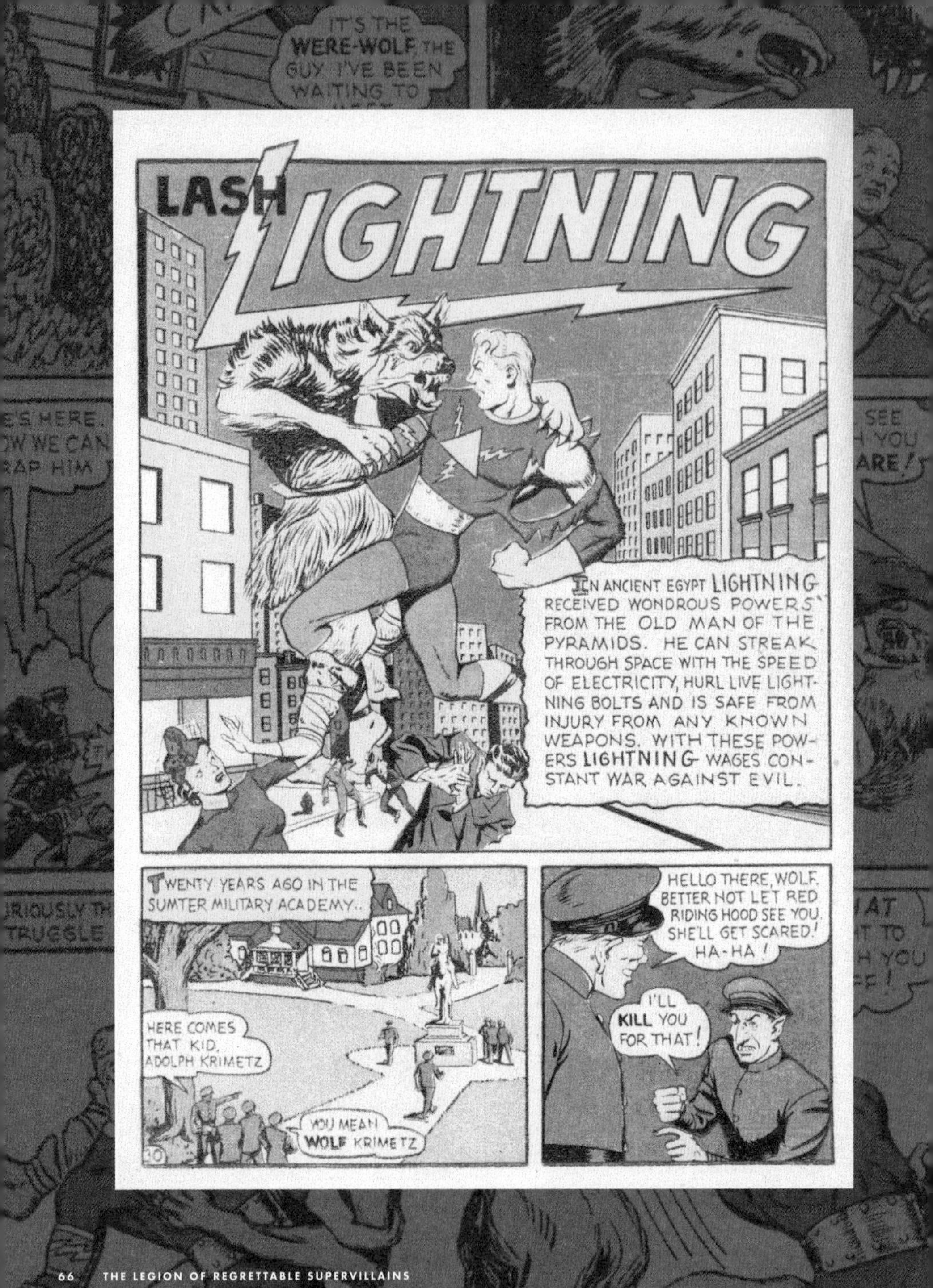

LASH LIGHTNING

IN ANCIENT EGYPT LIGHTNING RECEIVED WONDROUS POWERS FROM THE OLD MAN OF THE PYRAMIDS. HE CAN STREAK THROUGH SPACE WITH THE SPEED OF ELECTRICITY, HURL LIVE LIGHTNING BOLTS AND IS SAFE FROM INJURY FROM ANY KNOWN WEAPONS. WITH THESE POWERS LIGHTNING WAGES CONSTANT WAR AGAINST EVIL.

THE WERE-WOLF

"No one can show horror at my appearance and live!"

ARE BAD GUYS BORN that way, or is it an uncaring, often critical world which transforms innocent babes into murderous maniacs? There's a strong case to be made for both scenarios regarding Adolph Krimetz. Born with oversized canine teeth, pointy ears, and a wolf-like nature, he found himself the recipient of constant harassment from jeering peers and frightened passers-by. That Krimetz eventually transformed into a full-fledged werewolf and started murdering people comes as practically no surprise at all. (Well . . . maybe it's a *little* bit of a surprise.)

Trouble starts when, while a military cadet, Krimetz takes violent offense at a fellow student addressing him with the nickname "Wolf Krimetz." Viciously assaulting his heckler, Krimetz comes out of his rage and is shocked to discover that the boy is dead due to a sudden case of having his skull cracked against a nearby tree. Krimetz relocates to a hidden cave in the distant mountains, where he "grows into a shaggy beast of a man nursing hate, vengeance, and rebellion at his fate." Eventually his thoughts of revenge turn towards the high-ranking United States military officers who were once his fellow cadets.

Initially, Krimetz plants bombs, but when that fails he unleashes his real power. "From the waist up," cries a caption in alarm, "he becomes a real wolf!" It's an atypical type of lycanthropy, but it works for Krimetz, who discovered while in isolation that his lupine features were the result of having been born a werewolf!

The Were-Wolf can bend steel bars with ease, survive tremendous falls, and has few weaknesses. But a direct shot of electricity can force him to return to his human form. This is unfortunate for him, since his superheroic nemesis is Lightning, a human dynamo gifted with the power to control electricity in addition to his tremendous strength and power of flight.

After several tussles across a handful of stories, Krimetz begins seeking a cure. As doctors either recoil in horror or attempt to turn him over to the authorities, Krimetz goes on a killing spree throughout hospitals and medical centers. In a final confrontation with Lightning, the Were-Wolf loses his footing and plunges into the dark, choking depths of a factory smokestack.

VS

Enemy of:
Lightning

Created by:
Mark Schneider and an uncredited writer

Debuted in:
Four Favorites #1 (Ace Comics, September 1941)

Known weaknesses:
Fleas, baths, the mailman

ZOR THE CAVEMAN

"Now Zor beat you!"

Enemy of:
Midnight

Created by:
Jack Cole

Debuted in:
Smash Comics #38 (Quality Comics, December 1942)

Preferred weapons:
Spiked club; excruciating grammar

IT'S AN UNFORTUNATE FACT that people tend to judge a book by its cover. And in the case of a brutish but gentle giant manipulated by civilized but secretly sinister types, this makes for a tragic story.

When Zor's saga begins, the city is alight with anticipation over Sir Squinchworth's return from Siberia with a phenomenal find. Standing next to a steel-barred cage, the officious Squinchworth tells the assembled crowd: "You are gazing at a living specimen of neanderthal man! Fifty thousand years old! Discovered by myself frozen in a Siberian glacier! And when he was thawed out, came to life, unbelievable as it seems!!"

It does seem unbelievable. But Zor—hulking and furious—stands in the cage for all to see. Roaring with outrage, the primitive man escapes his captivity and storms the crowd, sending the city into a panic. "He's a killer!" someone cries quite unnecessarily as Zor chases the crowd with a spiked club.

The neanderthal's actions at the nearby zoo don't do much to salvage his reputation. He liberates, defeats, and consumes a leopard in short order. It's after this that Zor is discovered by Midnight, and much to the crime fighter's surprise—Zor is comfortably dozing under a tree. "Why, he's peaceful as a dove!" Midnight notices, shocked. "Something tells me the poor devil was purposefully starved to make him vicious!"

He's very much right! While Zor remains missing, Squinchworth delights at the thought of the high price his pet caveman will bring when recovered. He's particularly excited by an offer of $40,000 from "Dingling Brother's" circus, noting "When he's recaptured, his value will be doubled!"

But Zor isn't recaptured anytime soon. Two months later, the "caveman" has been rehabilitated, taught to speak, and is ready to avenge himself on his former master. Narrowly avoiding a savage beating, Squinchworth takes refuge with a stern, female partner he addresses only as "Mama." But Zor knows neither fear nor etiquette—he knocks her out with one punch!

Cornered and stricken by conscience, Squinchworth swallows a bottle of sleeping pills and confesses his crimes, releasing the inhabitants of a locked cell from their imprisonment. "Meet my homemade freaks!" he wails, "Leopard boy, Long-Neck, Mick Midget, and 'Heady' Lamarr. All normal children a few years ago, but binding, growth control and special diets made them freaks!"

It was the same process by which he created Zor, now reformed. In addition to freeing his prisoners and confessing his crimes, Squinchworth also goes to jail—he mistakenly took indigestion tablets rather than sleeping pills!

DECEMBER
NO.38

SMASH
COMICS

10¢

FLIP THE COVER AND SEE WHAT HAPPENS TO *MIDNIGHT*!

DON'T DO IT, FOLKS.. THE CAVEMAN IS INSIDE!

BEETLE
RUN, JUANITA! I CAN'T STOP THIS THING!
HAS THE MIGHTY BLUE BEETLE FINALLY MET HIS MATCH IN THE TERRIBLE... "PRAYING MANTIS-MAN"?
JAGUAR
JAN. 1962
JAGUAR! EITHER YOU BECOME THE SERVANT OF THE CAT-GIRL ... OR I'LL ORDER MY LIVING SPHINXES TO DESTROY YOUR EXPLORER FRIENDS!
MY ANSWER IS NO CAT-GIRL! I WILL NEVER SERVE YOU EVIL SCHEMES!
INTO THE LIFE OF THE JAGUAR APPEARS THE AMAZING CAT-GIRL, LEGENDARY RULER OF FELINE CREATURES! DOES THIS DANGEROUS BEAUTY BECOME FRIEND OR FOE OF THE MASTER OF THE ANIMAL KINGDOM IN THE STARTLING STORY OF ....
The RETURN of the CAT-GIRL!
AMERICA
THE POWER OF-- BULLDOZER
EXTRA! THE ORIGIN OF MODOK!
MAD-NESS
BLACK CA
NO. 28 APRIL
THE DARLING OF COMICS
CAN THE BLACK CAT OUTWIT THE PHANTOM BUCCANEER AND AVENGE THE INNOCENT VICTIMS OF AN AGE-OLD CURSE? READ:
THE CRIMSON RAIDER!

PART 2

The SILVER AGE 1950–1969

AS SUPERHERO COMICS EMERGED FROM their troubled adolescence, they discovered a newfound popularity that rivaled their early appeal when the genre was brand-new. Leading the charge was a new breed of hero, as likely to spend time pondering personal problems as to wade into battle with the baddies.

As the heroes got deeper, so did the villains. Gone were the days of random rogues who'd appear out of nowhere, snuff a few high-ranking government officials or some such, and then find themselves ironically assassinated by their own evil schemes. Supervillains now had backstories to rival those of the costumed crime fighters they clashed against. Industry veterans like Stan Lee, Carmine Infantino, Jack Kirby, Robert Kanigher, Steve Ditko, and many others began to create colorful casts of costumed crooks. These superfiends not only rivaled their foes for well-rounded characterization, but also became recurring characters in their own right. The supervillain had finally gained a level of stardom.

Whether they were Commie agents, ape overlords, or a new variety of gimmicked no-goodnik—or some combination of all three—supervillains were now popular enough to earn cover appearances, multi-issue storylines, and a little merchandising. They still tended to lose against the guy whose name graced the cover, but at least they got their licks in. With the postwar economic boom encouraging readers' interest in science, space flight, espionage, and industry, the supervillains of the Silver Age had no end of raw material to draw inspiration from. And have we mentioned all the apes?

NOTE: By some accounting, the Silver Age of comics started in the mid-1950s, separated from the Golden Age by a few years of artistic stagnation.

ANIMAL-VEGETABLE-MINERAL MAN

"I have succeeded in duplicating that process—of creating life artificially!"

Enemy of:
The Doom Patrol

Created by:
Arnold Drake and Bruno Premiani

Debuted in:
Doom Patrol vol. 1, #89 (DC Comics, August 1964)

Only thing missing:
The kitchen sink

PART OF THE APPEAL of superhero comics is the limitless range of superpowers characters can possess. Transform into a tiger? Control the elements? Snake your limbs around an adversary like a clinging vine? Everything is possible!

And, in some instances, a lucky character is loaded with practically every superpower in the book. Such is the case with Animal-Vegetable-Mineral Man, a villain with a mouthful of a name and a list of abilities as lengthy as the Oxford English Dictionary.

When the future Animal-Vegetable-Mineral Man first appears, he's a mild-mannered but brilliant scientist named Sven Larsen. A onetime student of Niles Caulder (aka "the Chief," leader and founder of the superheroic Doom Patrol), Larsen had maintained a grudge against his former instructor for years. But he visits Caulder, seemingly to make amends.

Also on Larsen's agenda is a demonstration of his new scientific discovery. "According to our latest theory of the origin of life," he explains, "it began when amino acids—complex chemical compounds floating in our barren seas—were bombarded by lightning!" Standing astride a metal walkway over a bubbling pit—rarely a good idea in comics—Larsen gets to the juicy bit. "I have succeeded in duplicating that process—*of creating life artificially!*" Perched mere feet over his swirling concoction, he barely has time to explain his process before promptly falling directly into the churning soup.

Those are the last words Larsen speaks, but the results of his chemical bath do the talking for him. Emerging as a giant malevolent paramecium, the transformed Larsen creates a path of wanton destruction. As if to prove his varied talents, he rapidly cycles through a series of bizarre transformations, from paramecium to sulphur giant to creeping ivy to titanic bird. (His most famous look is the bizarre amalgam shown on the cover: part man, part dinosaur, part crystal, part tree. Modestly adorned in a blue leotard.) Caulder declares: "Is it animal, vegetable or mineral . . . it's all three!" That's some good science.

It becomes clear that Larsen's grudge against the Chief is anything but settled. Ironically, it's the cause of their feud—an "anti-decay ray" which he claims Caulder stole—that proves the undoing of the Animal-Vegetable-Mineral Man. Larsen returns to his human form. Although he would later regain his mojo and returned to pester the Doom Patrol, Animal-Vegetable-Mineral Man provides a humbling lesson that a villain wielding such tremendous power was nonetheless undone by his own worst enemy—himself.

SUPERMAN
DC
NATIONAL COMICS
THE WORLD'S STRANGEST HEROES BATTLE A TRIPLE THREAT--THREE VILLAINS IN ONE--THE MAN WHO BECOMES
"The Animal-Vegetable-Mineral Menace!"
APPROVED BY THE COMICS CODE AUTHORITY
AUG. NO. 89
THE DOOM PATROL
12¢

CAPTAIN MARVEL in The RETURN OF ATOM-JAW
HAH! OF ALL THE NUMBSKULLS! ...TO THINK THEY CAN HOLD ME BEHIND BARS! WATCH!
ON THE 14TH OF FEBRUARY, ATOM-JAW THE INTERNATIONAL PIRATE, ALMOST SUCCEEDED IN A PLOT TO FLOOD THE WORLD'S BLACK MARKETS WITH ISOTOPES AND SO DISCREDIT THE UNITED STATES' GOOD-NEIGHBOR POLICY! HE WAS STOPPED BY THE VALIANT CAPTAIN MARVEL AND THEN TURNED OVER TO THE COAST GUARD.
AT THIS MOMENT, ATOM-JAW IS LOCKED IN THE BRIG OF THE COAST GUARD CUTTER...
SNAP!

ATOM-JAW

"I wanted this to be a personal battle, Captain Marvel, and now it begins!"

MITATION IS, AS THEY say, the sincerest form of flattery. That being said, Atom-Jaw is practically obsequious in his mirrorlike resemblance to one of the Golden Age's most persistent and visually striking villains.

Iron Jaw was the recurring nemesis of boy vigilante Crimebuster. Under his thick brow and beady black eyes he bore a terrifying, jagged prosthetic mandible. He resembled a cross between a shark and a killer robot. Serving Hitler directly as America's premier fifth columnist, Iron Jaw was also a vicious gangster, harassing not only Crimebuster but, occasionally, other characters in the company's lineup.

But the very similarly appointed villain who populated M.F. Enterprise's *Captain Marvel* comics wasn't Iron Jaw. He was the atom age equivalent (or, to be less generous, the blatant copy): Atom-Jaw!

Atom-Jaw frequently fought the superheroic, limb-splitting alien robot Captain Marvel—with "frequently" being a relative term. This Captain Marvel was neither the Shazam!-spouting, red-suited hero who has served with the Justice League, nor the space-spanning superwoman who's been attached to the Avengers. Rather, he was a short-lived knockoff in a maroon suit who appeared in only six comic books. Still, for as briefly as this Captain Marvel exercised the use of the name, Atom-Jaw was there to fight him.

Prior to the start of his criminal career, Atom-Jaw had been one Dr. Preston, an atomic scientist who'd survived a terrible nuclear explosion that claimed his lower jaw. Fortunately—more or less—skilled surgeon Dr. Safion was able to craft a snaggletoothed metal prosthetic using experimental material Compound X-4. Unsurprisingly, Preston wasn't exactly delighted when the bandages came off. Dr. Safion, recalling the dramatic moment, says, "He bit everything in sight! He was like a human barracuda, *but worse*!"

Atom-Jaw's atomic jaw can, indeed, bite through any known material. In addition to Dr. Safion's list, which includes "steel bars, brick walls, chairs," the metal-mandibled menace has been known to bite through lampposts, cars, and boats! He does have his limits, though. "I'm not a cannibal" he tells his arresting officer, "I'd never use my teeth on a human!" Perhaps that's why he was so comfortable chomping away at the android Captain Marvel.

Enemy of:
Captain Marvel

Created by:
Roger Elwood, Leon Francho, and Carl Burgos

Debuted in:
Captain Marvel #2 (M.F. Enterprises, June 1966)

Sense of humor:
Not as biting as you'd expect

CAT GIRL

"Gaze upon me in wonder!"

Enemy of:
The Jaguar

Created by:
Robert Bernstein and John Rosenberger

Debuted in:
Adventures of the Jaguar #4 (Archie Comics, January 1962)

Favorite luxury car:
Take a guess

THERE'S A THIN LINE, as they say, between love and hate. Even in the often-chaste world of superhero comics, passion can overrule principles, leading to occasions when a hyper-heart drives the super-brain, rather than the other way around. Not immune to this is Cat Girl, a villain whose heady pedigree of power is motivated more by romance than by larceny.

Immortal and worshipped by all feline creatures great and small since the age of the pharaohs, Cat Girl made a profound impression on the ancient world. Theoretically, both the myth of the Sphinx and the famous structure that bears its name were based upon her (despite the fact that she doesn't possess a lion's body—artistic license, one supposes).

Cat Girl possesses the power to command cats and other feline creatures, as well as to fly and perform feats of tremendous strength (plus a handful of other abilities that pop up as they're needed). Also among her arsenal: a very specific but effective ability to command the stone monuments of the so-called Valley of the Sphinxes, a recently discovered site where a half dozen smaller replicas of the larger construction lie around, awaiting their mistress's command.

But for all that, she finds herself powerless before the wiles of the Jaguar. Possessing powers basically equal to those of Cat Girl, the valorous Jaguar has the benefit of being "the world's most attractive bachelor," as the text repeatedly insists. What's a Cat Girl to do? It's no wonder that while trying to conquer the world, she can't help but get giddy in the presence of such a superheroic hunk.

In fact, she's not alone. Throughout his career, the Jaguar frequently faces femmes fatales whose aims include canoodling along with world-conquering. Kree-Nal, a silver-haired and green-skinned beauty billed as "the Sea Circe from Space," also has the hots for the Jag, as does the husband-seeking intergalactic tyrant Tola!

Cat Girl repeatedly bumps heads with the Jaguar, slowly warming to the side of good with each defeat. Eventually, both she and the emerald-hued Kree-Nal become his allies. Joining with Jill Ross, the love-struck secretary of the Jaguar in his civilian identity, the trio are declared the New Jaguar Rescue Team and tasked with protecting the world in the event the Jaguar should ever meet his end. In sponsoring this assemblage, the Jaguar may have created every superguy's worst nightmare: a team comprised entirely of his ex-girlfriends!

ARCHIE ADVENTURE SERIES
ADVENTURES OF
The JAGUAR
APPROVED BY THE COMICS CODE AUTHORITY
12¢
PDC
MAY
THE WORLD'S MOST ATTRACTIVE BACHELOR IS THE JAGUAR! MILLIONS OF GIRLS IDOLIZE HIM, INCLUDING THE GLAMOROUS, DANGEROUS CAT GIRL! WATCH THE FUR FLY AS THE JAGUAR FALLS FOR THE
CAT GIRL'S RIVAL

INTRODUCING BLACK CAT'S NEW ALLY, KIT, FEARLESS BOY SENSATION!

BLACK CAT

NO. 28 APRIL

PDC

THE DARLING OF COMICS

IT'S A HARVEY COMICS HIT!

CAN THE BLACK CAT OUTWIT THE PHANTOM BUCCANEER AND AVENGE THE INNOCENT VICTIMS OF AN AGE-OLD CURSE? READ:

THE CRIMSON RAIDER!

10c

THE CRIMSON RAIDER

"??!" [The Crimson Raider doesn't speak, except for this confused punctuation.]

IS IT POSSIBLE TO pity the villain? This is the question posed by the Crimson Raider, a pirate so evil that he was cursed by the Devil himself to toil fruitlessly in the living world . . . and to become an unwieldy giant in the bargain!

The Crimson Raider was an alias for Al Gory, a vicious pirate "known and feared on the seven seas." Despite his terrifying reputation, Gory was no less susceptible to violence than the next man. Ambushed while disembarking his ship, the Raider dies on the docks having never even drawn his cutlass. Since a lifetime of high-seas piracy rendered Gory unfit for celestial glory, he is promptly turned away from the Pearly Gates. Wandering downstairs, however, he finds that he's not wanted even in the fiery underworld.

"He was told," explains an old crone as she relates the story, "should he be able to locate an honest namesake to whom he could turn over his ill-gotten booty, one who would use these riches for the betterment of mankind, he would then be allowed to serve out his term of penance" in the bowels of hell. Why anyone would work so hard to get where the Crimson Raider was heading is a mystery. Perhaps the rent was cheap.

Back in the mortal world, Gory gathered and hid his prodigious fortune of gold ducats and spent decade after decade seeking someone who shares his surname so he could hand off the treasure. Invariably, though, the vast wealth would corrupt the recipient. Which meant Gory had to re-collect every coin of the treasure and start the process over again.

This required a few murders along the way. But a hidden condition of Satan's deal made that easier with each failure: Gory grew a foot taller every time he failed to resolve the curse. After three hundred years of bad choices, the Crimson Raider was now a titanic giant, leaving corpses of his victims scattered across the tops of telephone poles or on cliff sides.

When Hollywood's Glamorous Detective Star, Linda Turner—aka the Black Cat—and her sidekick Kit become involved with the mystery, they easily make short work of the giant. Pelting him with rocks, dodging his mighty blows, and even causing the colossus to clothesline himself on telephone wires, the Black Cat and Kit confront him at the site of his hidden treasure. A crumbling cliff seals the Raider's doom, as he plummets to the beach and lands upon his own giant-size cutlass.

"Gone for good" muses the Black Cat, "his terrible wanderings ended by his own cutlass!" Whether this means he ever found peace or torment in the →

VS

Enemy of:
The Black Cat and Black Kitten

Created by:
Lee Elias and Bob Haney

Debuted in:
Black Cat #28 (Harvey Comics, April 1951)

Day job:
Paul Bunyan impersonator

afterlife is unclear. For all we know, the Crimson Raider just had to start all over again, twelve inches taller this time . . .

ROLL CALL...

Other gigantic no-goodniks include supersized supervillains like Giganta, a frequent foe of both Wonder Woman and the Super Friends. Atlas, formerly "Power Man" and "the Smuggler," was an ionically amped supervillain who made a go at reforming later in his career, while King-Size fought for "giants' rights." Most dynamic of the giant villains may have been the Claw—a fang-toothed, goblinlike sometimes-ally of the Axis powers who frequently clashed with Golden Age superheroes Daredevil, the Silver Streak, and the Ghost!

LINDA TURNER, HOLLYWOOD STAR AND AMERICA'S SWEETHEART, BECOMES BORED WITH HER ULTRA-SOPHISTICATED LIFE OF MOVIE MAKE-BELIEVE AND TAKES TO CRIME-FIGHTING IN HER MOST DRAMATIC ROLE OF ALL AS THE...
BLACK CAT
STRANGE AND TERRIBLE IS THE TALE OF THE PHANTOM BUCCANEER WHO TERRIFIED A COUNTRY-SIDE, SPREADING FEAR AND HORROR UNTIL THE NEMESIS OF CRIME–THE BLACK CAT AND HER NEW ALLY, KIT, INTERCEDED TO BATTLE...
"The CRIMSON RAIDER!"

GENERALISSIMO BRAINSTORM

"Heed my mental command, Pirana—drop your weapon! You are my prisoner!"

Enemy of:
Pirana

Created by:
Otto Binder and Jack Sparling

Debuted in: *Thrill-O-Rama* #2 (Harvey Comics, September 1966)

Number of troops he commands:
Depends if you count attack dolphins and mechanical mermaids

SQUAT, ROUND, AND POSSESSED of a shiny bald noggin that resembles a large, pink lightbulb, Generalissimo Brainstorm makes up for his short stature with a fancy uniform and spectacular psychic powers that make him the greatest mental menace on the high seas (possibly the only mental menace on the high seas).

His opponent: underwater superhero Pirana. Although superheroes are no strangers to lucky accidents, Pirana takes the "stumbled into superpowers" cake. While testing a revolutionary "super-thin piece of transparent silicone rubber" designed to extract oxygen from water, Pirana *gets it stuck to his face.* With the membrane permanently fused over his mouth and nose, he can breathe only when submerged in water. Luckily, he is a "glass half full" type of guy and decides to wage war against evil under the sea.

Though oceans cover most of the world's surface, it's only a matter of time before Pirana crosses path with the submarine-borne Generalissimo. He's hard to miss. Brainstorm's mighty mind creates electrical "brainstorms," which send sparks and sizzling stars into a frenetic orbit around his extra-large forehead. This grants him increased intelligence, telepathy, and mind control. He refers to the latter power as his "crackle command," which sounds very much like a brand of sugary children's cereal. Appropriate, since the sound effect of Brainstorm's brainstorms is "Snap," "Crackle," "Pop!"

Brainstorm employs a collection of sinister sidekicks. His head scientist, Chief Ooz, provides the services of a specially trained attack dolphin, "his porpoise with a deadly purpose." And the Human Anchor, like his namesake, exhibits the powers of sinking and getting stuck in the sand.

Lastly, there's Murderina Mermaid, "the most complex machine ever developed," reads her introductory caption, adding snidely, "mainly because she's a woman." Murderina's wind-up womanly wiles come closest to preparing a twitterpated Pirana for a fatal fall.

Generalissimo Brainstorm's second big scheme is the most delightfully insane plan ever concocted by any brain, superpowered or not. "First," he says, preparing to utter sentences never spoken before or since by any living being, "charges will blow open the pens that harbor Gibraltar's famous pet apes." As if you didn't need all afternoon to parse that statement, he adds: "Then, in the confusion, the bank at its base holding world-wide funds will be raided!" Just repeating that first sentence aloud would probably cause confusion enough, General.

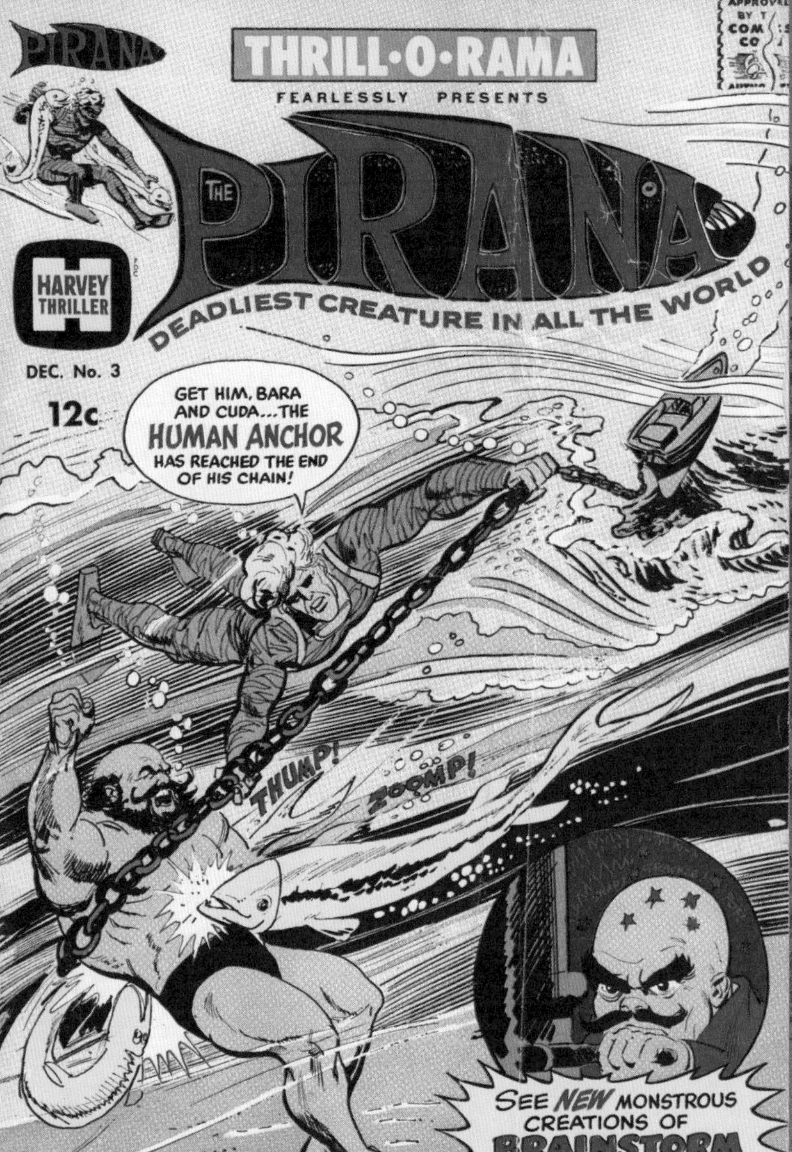
PIRANA
THRILL-O-RAMA
FEARLESSLY PRESENTS
THE PIRANA
DEADLIEST CREATURE IN ALL THE WORLD
HARVEY THRILLER
DEC. No. 3
12c
GET HIM, BARA AND CUDA... THE HUMAN ANCHOR HAS REACHED THE END OF HIS CHAIN!
THUMP!
ZOOMP!
SEE NEW MONSTROUS CREATIONS OF BRAINSTORM WORLD'S MOST BRILLIANT VILLAIN!

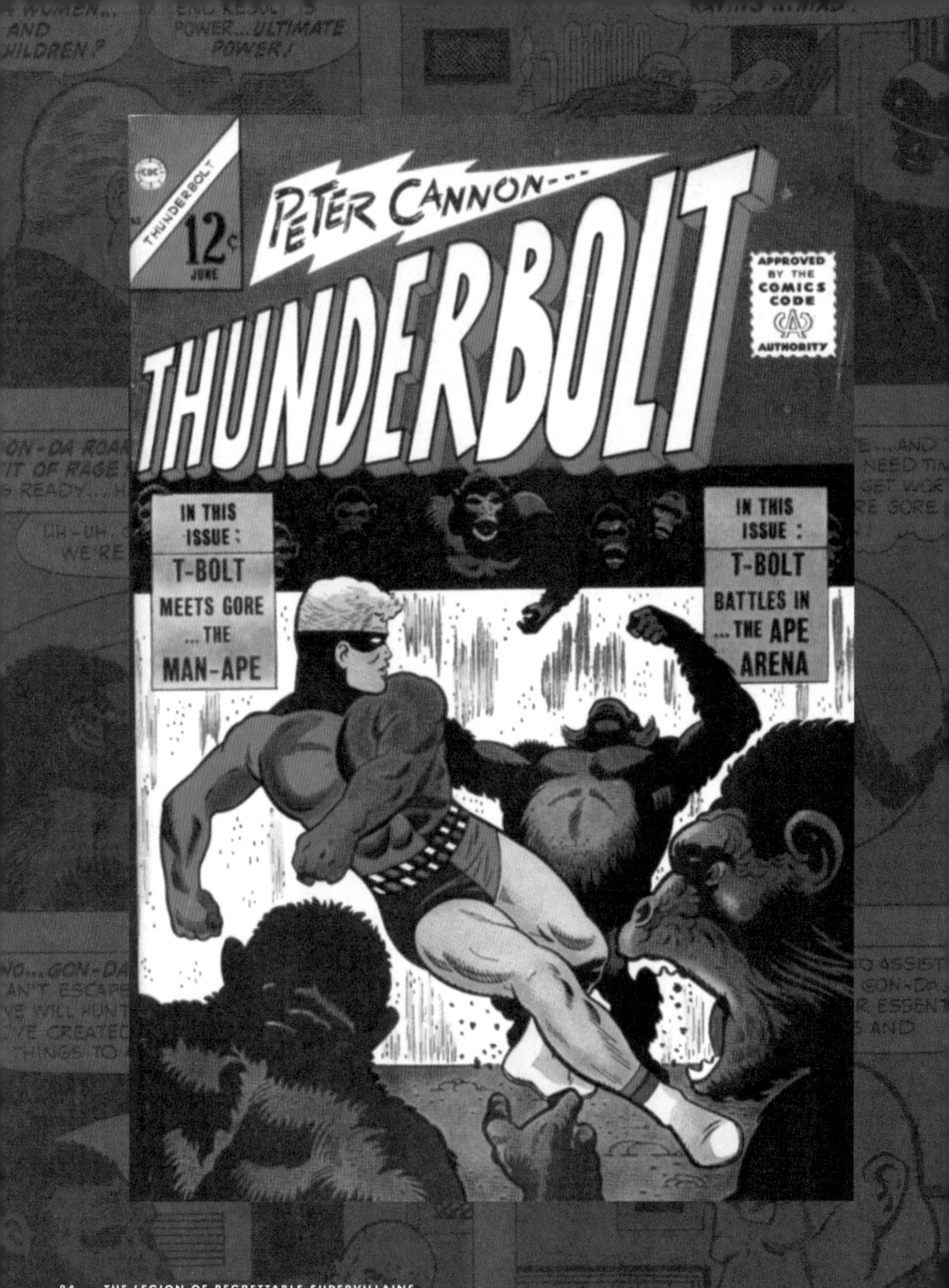

THUNDERBOLT
12¢
JUNE

PETER CANNON---
THUNDERBOLT

APPROVED BY THE COMICS CODE AUTHORITY

IN THIS ISSUE: T-BOLT MEETS GORE ... THE MAN-APE

IN THIS ISSUE: T-BOLT BATTLES IN ... THE APE ARENA

GORE THE MAN-APE

"The law? Ha! I am the law on Gore Island!"

SOME TYRANTS RULE WITH an iron fist. In the case of Eric Gore, a chrome-domed dictator on a remote island populated only by an army of apes, it was less an iron fist and more a monkey's paw.

Literally: Gore's left hand was replaced with that of a gorilla, inexplicably granting him the authority to control an island full of the powerful primates. The situation is a mixed bag, but Gore has no one to blame but himself. A medical specialist experimenting on advanced skin-grafting techniques, Gore was caught in a powerful explosion. He loses his hand (and sight in one eye), and then: "I heard the dying groan of an experimental ape, injured in the blast," explains Gore. "I operated then and there, and transferred the creature's paw . . . and was successful!"

While the operation granted him a replacement for his missing mitt, there were—as he says—"unforeseen complications." Over the subsequent weeks of healing, Gore experiences strange sensations and a burning desire for power. "I knew then," he tells us, "that the humanity I had sacrificed to serve . . . would one day serve me!" Gore sets himself up on a remote island and, in a lucky stroke, discovers that it is home to a tribe of impressionable apes. "The dumbfounded creatures mistook my appearance for that of a god, and proclaimed me their supreme ruler!" How he knows that for a fact isn't particularly clear, but Gore seems like the kind of man who fills in the blanks.

From his sinister headquarters deep in the jungles of his secluded island, Gore plans to take over the world using flesh-eating chemical weapons. With the cooperation of the local gorillas. "A small army of apes will be my initial striking force," he crows, "but they will grow as the criminal elements flock to my side!" It's a good enough plan but, unfortunately for Gore, reluctant superhero Peter Cannon—aka Thunderbolt—is accidentally shipwrecked on the nearby reefs. Bad news for the apes; by the end of the story, Thunderbolt has punched a whole bunch of them in their individual monkey faces. Thunderbolt also volunteers to fight in Gore's arena, standing in for human victims. Facing four "mad apes," he is observed by an audience of primates politely seated on wooden bleachers as though they were attending a rodeo of some sort.

Naturally, Thunderbolt defeats his ape adversaries. By happy circumstance, this also disinclines the wild tribe to obey the further commands of Eric Gore, ape hand or no ape hand. The would-be tyrant ends up perishing in an explosion, a definitive end for the unlikely villain. Unless he was able to survive and attach more ape parts to his explosion-battered body . . .

VS

Enemy of:
Peter Cannon, Thunderbolt

Created by:
Peter A. Morisi

Debuted in:
Peter Cannon, Thunderbolt #52 (Charlton Comics, June 1966)

Handedness:
Ape

GIGANTA

Created by:
William Moulton Marston and H. G. Peter

Debuted in:
Wonder Woman vol. 1, #9 (DC Comics, June 1944)

Her statuesque frame, rolling locks of shocking red hair, and glamorous leopard-print two-piece might make the exceptionally tall Giganta seem like a human woman. But in fact she is a super-evolved ape. Driven up the evolutionary ladder by an experimental machine that sends the entire world into a prehistoric state of grace, the clever and vicious Giganta takes the opportunity to try to convince the people of the primordial world to choose evil over good. Luckily Wonder Woman is there to stop her!

THE GORILLA BOSS OF GOTHAM CITY

Created by:
David V. Reed, Lew Sayre Schwartz and Charles Paris

Debuted in:
Batman vol. 1, #75 (DC Comics, February 1953)

Mobster George Dyke is executed for his crimes, but his henchmen retrieve his body from the gas chamber. With his brain placed inside the skull of a giant ape, the titanic beast embarks on a crime spree around Batman's hometown of Gotham City. Despite his power, he is ultimately defeated and—adding insult to injury—assorted aliens come by later on to steal his brain and use it for weird space experiments.

THE GORILLA WITCH

Created by:
Dave Wood and Bernard Bailey

Debuted in:
Strange Adventures #186 (DC Comics, March 1966)

Jungle explorer Reed Upton sets out to discover a strange serum that should grant him "mental contact with all forms of animal life." What he discovers instead is a scheming gorilla named Taro. Using the bubbling serum to turn Upton into a mindless ape and transform himself into an intellectual giant, Taro sets out to conquer the world! The evil ape disguises himself as Upton in order to acquire rare chemicals for his ape army, but his scheme is unraveled because he wears Upton's eye patch on the wrong eye. Apparently he's only so smart.

KING KRYPTON

Created by:
Otto Binder and Wayne Boring

Debuted in:
Action Comics #238 (DC Comics, March 1958)

When Superman and his pal Jimmy Olsen stumble across a giant, golden, superpowered ape in the wilds of Africa, the Man of Steel jumps to the likeliest conclusion: Kryptonian scientists must have rocketed the ape to Earth! Well, joke's on you, Supes: the ape *is* a Kryptonian scientist who accidentally turned a de-evolution ray on himself. So his friends put him in a rocket ship in hopes that being lost in space might cure him. Anyway, he turns back into a person just before dying, a real mess all around.

Historians disagree which legendary editor said it first, but it's an accepted truism that "Apes sell comics." Publishers with an eye on the bottom line couldn't help but notice that putting a monkey or a gorilla on a comic book cover increased sales dramatically.

THE MANDRILL

Created by:
Carole Seuling and Ross Andru

Debuted in:
Shanna the She-Devil #4 (Marvel Comics, June 1973)

Jerome Beechman had the misfortune of being born with baboonlike features, an appearance that subjected him to lifelong torment. On the other hand, his mutation also gave him the power to control women with his pheromones, so there's an upside. Assembling an all-woman army to conquer the world and partnering with a vampirelike villainess named Nekra, he is subsequently defeated by jungle heroine Shanna the She-Devil. He has returned a few times, only to be defeated anew by different heroes. Poor little monkey.

THE HUMAN FLYING FISH

"Now for another perfect getaway! I'll leapfrog high over Aquaman's sea creatures!"

Enemy of:
Aquaman

Created by:
Robert Bernstein and Ramona Fradon

Debuted in:
Adventure Comics #272 (DC Comics, May 1960)

Not to be confused with:
The Flying Human Fish; the Fishy Flying Human

A FINE STRATEGY FOR OVERCOMING a particular foe is to acquire the very same powers and abilities your enemy has—plus one more. This is the very specific and probably short-sighted logic behind the creation of the Human Flying Fish, a villain so remarkable that he deserves two adjectives in his nom du crime!

This fish story begins with Dr. Krill and his associate, Victor Bragg. Witnessing, from a lighthouse vantage point, the heroics of suboceanic lawmen Aquaman and Aqualad, the duo comes to a sobering conclusion about their crime careers. Namely that they don't stand a chance of stealing so much as a tin nickel while the King of the Sea and his young ward are out there patrolling the oceans.

But Dr. Krill has a plan. As he explains to his astonished young friend: "I'm not only an expert on medicine and marine life . . . I'm also an expert on Aquaman!"

The doctor reveals that what they need is someone whose powers are greater than Aquaman's. Inspired by a nearby school of flying fish, Krill proposes performing radical surgery to turn his partner into that someone. "You're an ex-swimming champ" he enthusiastically reminds Bragg, adding, "With your aquatic ability and my genius . . . we'll run a crime operation that Aquaman can't interfere with!"

Krill hijacks a hospital ship at sea and performs a shocking surgery. Soon Bragg possesses not only gills in addition to lungs—enabling him to breathe underwater—but remarkable speed both in and out of the ocean. Capable also of leaping over the water in powerful bounds, he can now easily escape Aquaman and his army of telepathically controlled sea creatures!

Unfortunately for Bragg, this is something of a one-note gimmick. While Aquaman can't follow the Human Flying Fish out of the water, he does arrange for a "net" of electric eels to shock the buoyant baddie into unconsciousness. Human Flying Fish or no Human Flying Fish, getting zapped by a living web of aquatic Tasers will knock the stuffing out of anyone. The Human Flying Fish has made a handful of reappearances since his debut, but some factor—maybe it's the name, maybe it's the costume, maybe it's the powers—keeps him from joining a regular stable of top-tier Aquafoes.

ADVENTURE COMICS

AQUAMAN

AMAZINGLY, A STRANGE PERSON SWIMS INTO AQUAMAN'S WATERY WORLD... TO CHALLENGE THE KING OF THE SEA! THIS NEW ARRIVAL CAN NOT ONLY MATCH AQUAMAN'S SWIMMING PROWESS, STROKE FOR STROKE, BUT HE HAS POWERS EVEN GREATER THAN AQUAMAN'S! HE CAN TRAVEL WHERE AQUAMAN CANNOT PURSUE HIM... INTO THE AIR! AND AQUAMAN CAN ONLY WATCH HELPLESSLY AS CRIMES ARE PILED UP BY THIS TRIPLE-THREAT VILLAIN OF LAND, SEA, AND AIR... THE MAN KNOWN AS...

The HUMAN FLYING FISH!

I CAN'T BELIEVE IT! MY SEA PATROL HAS SURROUNDED HIM! BUT HE'S FLYING RIGHT OVER THEIR HEADS! HE'S LIKE A FLYING FISH IN HUMAN FORM!

OFF THE ATLANTIC COAST ONE DAY, IN AN ABANDONED LIGHTHOUSE...

CAPT. FLASH

Once again, Captain Flash is called upon to match his wits and strength against his sworn enemy, The MIRROR MAN, in a battle of high stakes-- the lives of the world's foremost scientists...

The RETURN OF THE MIRROR MAN

MIRROR MAN

"Another foolish creature to nourish myself with!"

VS

F**OR MOST OF US,** a glance in the mirror reveals only our reflection. For Captain Flash, "defender of right and champion against evil," it reveals a menace from an alien realm!

"Out of the night it came to kill and destroy the greatest of mankind's scientific minds!" shouts a panicked caption in Mirror Man's debut. We're also warned that not only is Captain Flash unable to bring this "most terrifying of all foes" to justice, their duel will bring death to one of them!

That particular batch of hyperbole never pays off; both Captain Flash and Mirror Man walk away from their confrontations intact (spoiler alert). But the menace of Mirror Man is dire indeed. A leering, tentacled creature from an unknown dimension, he can produce himself from—or disappear into—any mirror. This gives him access to literally millions of locations around the Earth, although he makes his debut through a particularly unimpressive medicine chest in a men's public restroom. Perhaps he also needed to use the facilities.

Captain Flash, in his civilian identity of Keith Spencer (scientist at the Atom City Radiation Lab) is the first to recognize the threat of Mirror Man. Stumbling across one of the creature's victims, Flash skirmishes with Mirror Man and comes to an understanding of the creature's needs. "This Mirror Monster . . . whatever it is . . . needs silicon to live!" Why Mirror Man chooses to suck it from human bodies rather than gobbling up a sandy beach is anyone's guess.

In fact, Mirror Man is targeting "Earth's greatest minds." His reason isn't made clear, but when Captain Flash uses a convention of scientists as bait, Mirror Man slithers right into the trap. "I seldom have a selection of all the world's best scientific minds to choose my victims from," he gloats, just before the Captain flips a hidden switch and all the room's mirrors revolve back into the wall. All the luxuries of the modern bathroom!

Although the reflective rogue escapes, both Mirror Man and Captain Flash leave their final encounter looking forward to a third conflict. Mirror Man swears revenge, Captain Flash promises destruction, but we're all left hanging since another confrontation never occurred. Perhaps Earth ran out of brilliant scientific minds and Mirror Man took his business elsewhere.

Enemy of:
Captain Flash

Created by:
Mike Sekowsky and an uncredited writer

Debuted in:
Captain Flash #1 (Sterling Comics, November 1954)

Favorite Michael Jackson song:
"Man in the Mirror"

MODOK

"Once I was a mere guinea pig for the scientists of AIM! But, they did their job too well, and now I am their master!"

Enemy of:
Captain America, Iron Man, the Hulk, and more

Created by:
Stan Lee and Jack Kirby

Debuted in:
Tales of Suspense #93 (Marvel Comics, September 1967)

Hat size:
Men's Enormous

SUCCESS CAN GIVE EVEN the most grounded individual a swelled head. Imagine how much it went to the already-enlarged noggin of the hovering head of hate MODOK when he became the most popular oddball villain in comics history!

Although he debuted as a short-lived adversary to Captain America, MODOK has been pitted against practically every superhero in the Marvel Comics roster: the Sub-Mariner, the Hulk, Iron Man, Ms. Marvel, the Defenders, the Champions, Deadpool . . . you'd have an easier time listing every superhero whom MODOK has *never* struggled against than those he's already met. What seems to make MODOK so popular is the very thing that made him so often derided early in his career: the preposterous appearance of a giant head with tiny little arms and legs, flying around in a hoverchair, scowling and making pronouncements about his future domination of the planet. Since his debut, he's been transformed from a dour and self-important would-be world conqueror to a gleefully manic death machine, if not a hapless incompetent (despite the advantages of his huge head).

MODOK was originally George Tarleton, a lower-level scientist with the international cabal of evil scientists Advanced Idea Mechanics (known as AIM). The mutation resulting from an experiment in expanding human brainpower, he was originally dubbed MODOC: Mental Organism Designed Only for Computing. But his power grew with his ambition, and very soon he was operating the very branch of AIM that had created him. And his purpose changed from "Computing" to "Killing"!

Despite his apparent death—in fact, despite having died *multiple* times—MODOK returned repeatedly to harass every hero who crossed his path. His world-conquering ambitions often are sublimated, but they tend to hover below the surface. "One day I will rule this world," he admits in a more recent appearance. "And also win 'Dancing with the Stars.'" He was briefly replaced with his female equivalent, MODAM (Mental Organism Designed for Aggressive Maneuvers).

MODOK's appeal and audacity make him one of the most often invoked oddball villains, which seems to imply only great things for his future. He has already appeared in animation, video games, and merchandising—is it only a matter of time before MODOK comes to the movies? Let the stunt casting begin!

Ms. MARVEL TM

MARVEL® COMICS GROUP

35¢ 7 JULY 02198

©1977 MARVEL COMICS GROUP

Ms. MARVEL TM

I-I CAN'T RESIST HIS WILL! MODOK'S *FORCING* ME--TO KILL HER!

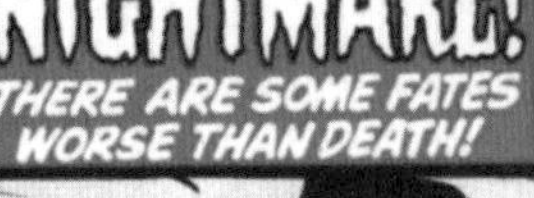

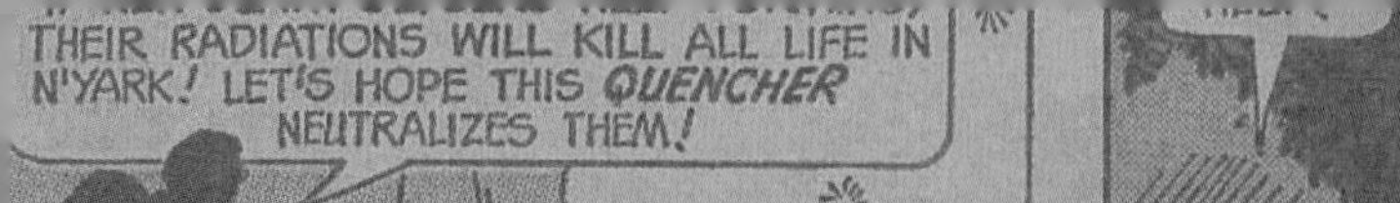

GOLD KEY

MIGHTY SAMSON

12c

MIGHTY SAMSON

10119-603 MARCH

High above N'Yark, Samson battles a fantastic man-creature whose strength matches his own!

OGGAR

"Oggar! Grrrrrr! Og-Garr!"

It's not uncommon to be of two minds about deep ethical quandaries. It's definitely rare, however, to have those conflicted feelings represented by a physical change from a normal human to a purple cat-monster.

The world into which Oggar is born is a postapocalyptic landscape overrun with bizarre menaces. There, the human race is isolated in the horror-ridden jungles of "N'Yark," once the greatest city on Earth and now a brutal landscape of hellish danger. So, in other words, not much has changed.

Protecting the ragtag bands of nearly savage survivors from varieties of mutated menace both large and small is Mighty Samson! Born with tremendous strength and imbued with equally tremendous courage, Samson defends what remains of humanity. When he and his companion Sharmaine scout the sites of deadly "Glow Geysers," which are erupting across the city, they discover a lone, unconscious human floating down the "Huz'n" river on a giant, mutated leaf. The man awakes with much of his memory missing, except for his name: Vaxar.

Soon after Vaxar's rescue, a new threat makes itself apparent, "an incredible brute even for a world where the fantastic is commonplace." This is Oggar, a towering, leonine figure sporting scaled legs and tail. Matching Samson in feats of strength, Oggar battles him with uprooted trees and traffic lights, and the two go toe-to-toe throwing loose, heavy postapocalypse junk at each other.

They are evenly matched, until Oggar breaks out his hidden power. "Can send thought commands to monsters," reveals the man-beast, finding spoken language highly difficult for his bestial vocal chords. He unleashes an array of mutant monstrosities: An armadillo-like "Rolling Monster" joins the giant "Dryland Clam" and a three-pronged attack consisting of a "magnetic eye monster," a "liquid beast," and a "flying swordfish."

It doesn't take Vaxar long to realize that *he* is Oggar, thanks to transformations triggered as a side effect of the otherwise-fatal Glow Geyser. At first, Vaxar only reluctantly helps protect his other self from danger, but soon he becomes a mostly willing accomplice to Oggar's terrible whims.

The ultimate clash between Oggar and Samson takes place on top of the still-standing Empire State Building . . . and concludes with Oggar plummeting to his doom, reverting to human form after death. Confused and saddened, the survivors briefly mourn their fallen friend. "Too bad his evil nature overcame him" says Sharmaine's father, Mindor, as Samson seals the Glow Geyser fissures. "Strange, to us the geysers were death . . . to him, life as a mutant man!"

Enemy of:
Mighty Samson

Created by:
Otto Binder and Frank Thorne

Debuted in:
Mighty Samson #5 (Western Publishing, March 1966)

Apt but unwieldy alternate name:
Inarticulate Purple Cat-Man Monster

PHANTASMON

"Lo! Now comes Phantasmon the Terrible! Bow down to your new master, Earthlings! Or pay the consequences!"

Enemy of:
Fly Man, Fly Girl, sophisticated New Yorkers

Created by:
Jerry Siegel and Paul Reinman

Debuted in:
Fly Man #35 (Mighty Comics Group, January 1966)

Greatest accomplishment:
Completely cleared sinuses

SOME SUPERVILLAINS ARE SIMPLY too powerful for a lasting career. If the hero and villain are significantly mismatched, the story of their battle tends to be very short. Take, as an example, Phantasmon. The "fearsome invader from outer space" shows up in the skies over New York, announcing his intent to conquer the Earth. "Sophisticated New Yorkers are flabbergasted—to put it mildly," explains a caption.

Decked out in a red devil costume and sporting a keenly trimmed goatee, Phantasmon seems to possess an array of powers unmatched in the history of comics. He is capable of transforming matter and commanding even inanimate objects to obey his wishes. He can fly, possesses "hyper-elasticity," and emits power-sapping rays from his fingers.

Most impressive, however, is Phantasmon's signature power, unduplicated in the annals of the medium: nasal lightning. "Behold," he cries unnecessarily, "lightning bolts . . . crashing out of my nostrils!"

Created by Jerry Siegel—cocreator of the hero who started it all, Superman—Phantasmon might make for an even match against the Man of Steel himself. Instead, he finds himself pitted against Fly Man and Fly Girl. Fly Man has a plan in case Phantasmon tries that lightning-from-the-nose trick again. "If he tries to fire any more bolts at us from his super-charged nose," he tells his partner, "bash him!"

Still, Phantasmon easily overpowers the heroes. And he didn't come alone. Despite his tremendous powers, Phantasmon chooses to delegate to his trio of bizarre and equally powerful subordinates: Sorro ("I have a genius for spreading misery," he explains), Disastro ("Wherever I roam, disaster is bound to rear its ugly head"), and the Crumbler—who sounds like the bad guy from a cookie commercial, but whose "mere presence can prove to be uniquely calamitous."

Fly Man hatches a last-ditch strategy. Contacting his most implacable enemies, "the dread amalgam known as Monsters Incorporated," Fly Man proposes a truce via a merciless foe known as the Iniquitous Bee-Man!

Agreeing that Monsters Incorporated should tackle Phantasmon "so they can't interfere with the plans of Earth Monsters against mankind," the hooded, scaly, densely furred, and incorporated monsters make surprisingly short work of the invaders. "Clever," Fly Girl tells Fly Man, "you conned Earth monsters into saving the Earth from alien monsters!" To which Fly Man can only reply hopefully, "And someday we'll defeat Monsters Incorporated, too!" Good luck with that.

SOME RE-UNION! ARE YOU SURPRISED? BUT WAIT, THERE ARE EVEN GREATER SURPRISES TO COME! MEANWHILE, SIT TIGHT, READ ON, AND THRILL TO THE AMAZING, SHOCKING ...
APPROVED BY THE COMICS CODE AUTHORITY
FLY MAN
12¢
MAC
MIGHTY COMICS GROUP
JAN. 1966
NO. 35
PHANTASMON THE TERRIBLE AND HIS ALIEOG-LABOIDS VS. FLY MAN & FLY GIRL

THE THOUSAND FOES OF THE SHIELD
THE ORIGIN OF THE BLACK HOOD

PHANTOM OF THE PENITENTIARY

"The Prison Phantom shall haunt these gray walls always . . . always . . . alwa—aaays . . ."

Enemy of:
The Hangman

Created by:
Jerry Siegel and Paul Reinman

Debuted in:
Mighty Comics #48 (Archie Comics, July 1967)

Locked away for:
Copycatting in the first degree

IN ADDITION TO MURDER, attempted murder, kidnapping, and unlawfully trespassing in a federal building, the elusive and murderous Phantom of the Penitentiary might add another crime to his rap sheet: copyright infringement.

Sporting a gorilla suit and a metal helmet, the so-called Phantom bears more than a passing resemblance to the titular character of the 1953 film *Robot Monster*. In fact, his shaggy gorilla suit and riveted metal helmet make for a nearly screen-accurate cosplay of the original.

Perhaps writer Jerry Siegel (who created Superman with artist Joe Shuster) knowingly based the Phantom on the B-movie monster. Siegel had a long history of mining old material for new characters. For example, comedians Danny Kaye and Joe E. Brown inspired Siegel and Shuster's superhero Funnyman and Superman's impish opponent Mr. Mxyzptlk, respectively. Even the Man of Steel himself owed a great deal to prior characters and stories, such as pulp hero Doc Savage and Philip Wylie's novel *The Gladiator.*

But back to the Phantom. "Haunting" Gothrak Penitentiary at nights, the bizarre figure slips into locked cells with ease, terrifying and assaulting the convicts—and sometimes the guards! Warden Amos Meggs, soon to retire, is more than happy to accept the help of the "macabre manhunter" known as the Hangman.

During the ensuing knock-down, drag-out battle, the Phantom seems flummoxed by the Hangman's prehensile rope ("Aieee!" the helmeted creature exclaims. "How can one kill the possessor of a crime-battling marvel-rope such as this?"). But then he escapes, leaving his metal helmet behind.

Later, in the warden's office, the Hangman insists—in a strange twist on the story of Cinderella—that every prison official try on the Phantom's helmet. His hunch that the so-called monster is in fact a disturbed member of the staff pays off: Former warden Meggs dons the helmet and immediately assumes the personality of the Phantom.

"The thought of going into forced retirement must have pushed him over the brink into mental illness," announces the Hangman, proud of his deductive abilities. "The victim of a split-personality, Meggs fashioned that costume and helmet—attacked those against whom he had fancied grievances!"

His secret exposed, Meggs will continue to haunt his own prison—but this time, from behind bars.

THE HANGMAN
WHEN THAT SWITCH REACHES THE BOTTOM ---
THE HANGMAN DIES..ELECTROCUTED BY THE PRISON PHANTOM! YOU DARED TO INVADE THIS PENITENTIARY.. WHICH IS MY DOMAIN! YOUR PENALTY..DEATH!!!
AGAIN AND AGAIN HAS THAT GRIMLY DEDICATED HUNTER OF WRONGDOERS, WHO IS KNOWN AS THE HANGMAN, CRUSHED THE INFERNAL PLOTS OF EVIL SCHEMERS! MANY ARE THE JAIL CELLS IMPRISONING CRIMINALS WHO WERE DRAGGED TO THE BAR OF JUSTICE BY THE LONE LAWMAN WHO GAVE THEM ENOUGH ROPE...WITH WHICH TO HANG THEMSELVES! BUT NOW THE MACABRE MANHUNTER WAGES HIS STRONGEST CONFLICT AGAINST HIS EERIEST FOE IN THE MOST UNEXPECTED SETTING OF ALL! LATCH ONTO THE UTMOST OF YOUR RAW COURAGE AND PLUMB THE UNGUESS-ABLE AS THE HANGMAN SPEEDS ALONG THE TWISTED TRAIL SPAWNED BY THE STALKING, BIZARRE TITAN OF TERROR KNOWN AS...
"THE PHANTOM OF THE PENITENTIARY!"
OUR LIVES ARE AT STAKE!
OOF!

BLUE BEETLE
12¢
JANUARY
BLUE BEETLE
APPROVED BY THE COMICS CODE AUTHORITY
RUN, JUANITA! I CAN'T STOP THIS THING!
HAS THE MIGHTY BLUE BEETLE FINALLY MET HIS MATCH IN THE TERRIBLE... "PRAYING MANTIS-MAN"?

SUPER-SONIC SPEED IT JETTED BACK TO THE GARDEN OF CRAWLING DEATH...

PRAYING MANTIS MAN

"One blast of my frigi-gun will end your meddling, Blue Beetle! You'll be stored in a bin in the slave-cave with all the others!"

Enemy of:
Blue Beetle

Created by:
Joe Gill and Bill Fraccio

Debuted in:
Blue Beetle #4 (Charlton Comics, January 1965)

What to do if encountered:
Pick him up with a tissue and gently deposit him outside

PITY THE NEW SUPERCROOK trying to invent an alias. With superhero comics having been around for decades, all of the good names are already taken. Thousands of superpowered types have already claimed their personally branded stake, so what remains are only the scraps.

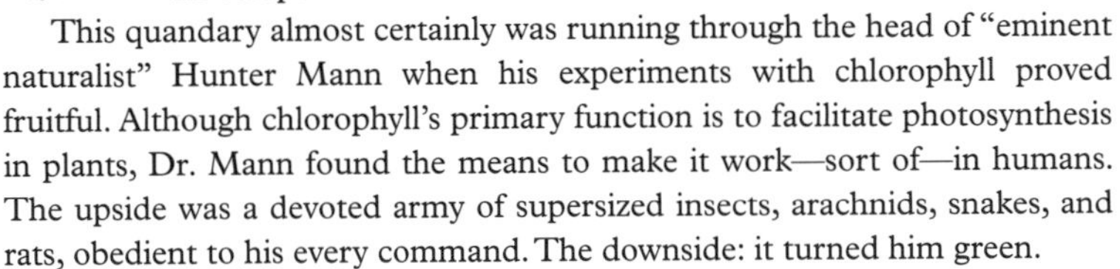

This quandary almost certainly was running through the head of "eminent naturalist" Hunter Mann when his experiments with chlorophyll proved fruitful. Although chlorophyll's primary function is to facilitate photosynthesis in plants, Dr. Mann found the means to make it work—sort of—in humans. The upside was a devoted army of supersized insects, arachnids, snakes, and rats, obedient to his every command. The downside: it turned him green.

It's either his fascination with creepy-crawlies or a slumped-shoulder surrender to his plant-hued pigmentation that encourages Dr. Mann to dress up like a six-foot cricket. The costume won't win awards for entomological accuracy, but it serves Mann's need for branding. Soon Praying Mantis Man overpopulates Baja, California, with enlarged beasties, drawing the attention of another chromatic insect type, the superheroic Blue Beetle. No pushover—at the time, Blue Beetle boasted the powers of superstrength, flight, and the ability to fire destructive blasts of energy—the Beetle is nonetheless initially overpowered.

Of course, he ultimately triumphs, and Praying Mantis Man is believed dead. But he returns, with giant army ants that assist Mann with his evil schemes and help out around the laboratory. If that weren't enough, he taught at least one of them to drive a car!

Praying Mantis Man barely spoke in his first appearance. But the second time around, he makes up for his silence by talking to himself nonstop. So we learn his ultimate scheme: "I am pursuing a logical plan," he insists to no one. "I am going to destroy man and the stupid civilization he has built!"

Praying Mantis Man is a formidable foe, but he exhibits one weakness: affection. After Blue Beetle has been frozen by Dr. Mann's devious "frigi-gun," the hero's quick-thinking girlfriend flatters Mann into giving her access to the steam valve that heats his underground headquarters. A thawed-out Beetle makes short work of PMM and his ant army. Still, insects are resilient. Who knows when Praying Mantis Man might come crawling back out from under the floorboards?

ROUND ROBIN

"I go wild when I'm close to money! Especially when it's somebody else's!"

Enemy of:
The Fighting American and Speedboy

Created by:
Joe Simon and Jack Kirby

Debuted in:
Fighting American #2 (Prize Comics, July 1954)

Favorite franchise restaurants:
Red Robin; Ground Round

LMOST INARGUABLY, THE GREATEST and best known creation of the long-running collaboration between Jack Kirby and Joe Simon is their shield-slinging superhero (and modern-day movie star) Captain America. When the duo revisited the concept during the height of the Cold War, however, their approach changed. Gone were the dire Axis baddies of World War II, and in their place was a coterie of comical criminals better suited to a carnival sideshow. (While the Fighting American began as a serious superhero, his satirical shift was, in part—according to Simon—a comical response to Senator Joseph McCarthy's witch hunt against alleged American Communists in 1954.)

Examples include one-man odd couple Double-Header, the League of the Handsome Devils, comical communist spies Hotsky Trotsky and Poison Ivan, and the bandit Yafata—who hides the secret of Yafata's Mustache.

Another such hoodlum was Round Robin, a corpulent crook whose means of escape often involved rolling down inclines at tremendous speeds. "There's never been a criminal of his type before! He's the fattest, trickiest, most untrustworthy devil of them all!" says patriotic hero the Fighting American. Tricky indeed. Before his debut story even begins, the "balloon-type scoundrel" and "sackful of sheer menace" has already robbed "Spiffany's" jewelry store; ransacked the vaults of Bagg, Burrow and Steele; and swiped the "solid gold underwear" off of Texas oil tycoon Yakima Fuldoon!

Capitalizing on a tap on the police commissioner's phone, Round Robin bounds out of nowhere and slams the Fighting American to the ground with one mighty bounce. "Jumping catfish!" swears the Fighting American. "This is like fighting with a mess of putty!"

Round Robin possesses a parcel of unusual abilities, though how he acquired them is never explained. His heroic opponents notice that the tubby terror can't be knocked out. "You haven't got any bones!" exclaims the Fighting American, delivering a mighty, two-fisted blow which only squashes the scallywag's skull harmlessly into his chest. "These rolls of fat cushion the force of the blows!"

In the end, the Fighting American figures out a clever scheme: Using a fleet of armored cars as bait, he traps Robin inside a truck filled to the brim with skin-stiffening starch! Once the bouncing baddie is as inflexible as a cue ball, he's easy to roll directly to jail.

THE ORIGINAL--ONE AND ONLY
FIGHTING AMERICAN
and SPEEDBOY
THERE'S NEVER BEEN A CRIMINAL OF HIS TYPE BEFORE! HE'S THE FATTEST, TRICKIEST, MOST UNTRUSTWORTHY DEVIL OF THEM ALL!
LOOK AT HIM GO! WE'VE NEVER KNOWN A CRIMINAL WHO RAN OUT ON US THIS WAY BEFORE!
FIGHTING AMERICAN AND SPEEDBOY
ROUND ROBIN!
JACK KIRBY

THE ASTONISHING
ANT-MAN!
IN..."the VENGEANCE of the SCARLET BEETLE!"
YOUR DAYS OF MEDDLING ARE ENDED, ANT-MAN! THE SCARLET BEETLE HAS VOWED TO DESTROY YOU!
GAMES
V-958
1
PLOT: STAN LEE • SCRIPT: LARRY LIEBER • ART: JACK KIRBY • INKING: DICK AYERS • LETTERING: A. SIMEK

THE SCARLET BEETLE

"At last you've met your match, Ant-Man!! Even you can't stop the hordes of the Scarlet Beetle!"

IT WOULD BE VERY unvillainlike for a menace to confront his foe on equal footing. Take, for instance, the evil Scarlet Beetle, who challenges the insect-themed and similarly small Ant-Man. Because he can literally face his opponent eye-to-compound-eye, the Beetle may not prove much of a menace to Ant-Man, who possesses his full human strength at even the tiniest size and commands an army of ants.

That's why the Scarlet Beetle deserves credit for stealing Ant-Man's size-altering gas and turning himself into a six-legged colossus!

The clash of tiny titans begins as Ant-Man is alerted by his loyal ants to some sort of insect menace brewing in the sewers of New York. He investigates and finds something of an insect political rally, with insects—"hundreds of them!"—gathered to listen to a talking, clearly intelligent red-hued beetle.

"For ages, the human race has ruled the Earth," the Scarlet Beetle tells the assembled throng, "but now, due to radiation which accidentally hit me during one of mankind's atomic experiments, I have been given a brain which is the equal of any human's!!"

"We insects, who number in the trillions," he continues, "shall seize control of the Earth from mankind!"

The Scarlet Beetle orders his followers to attack Ant-Man and, once in possession of the hero's canisters of size-changing gas, the Beetle enlarges himself to an intimidating size. Meanwhile, Ant-Man's captors place him in a small hole, which is a pretty good way to deal with him when you think about it. As the Beetle's armies sweep the Earth, they break down man's civilization. Termites collapse the communications network by chewing through telephone poles, spiders envenomate political leaders, bees disrupt television and radio stations, and presumably all the everyday creepy-crawlies show up just to ick everyone else out.

But Ant-Man escapes, and puts the offending insects to the rout. Subjecting the Beetle to a dose of shrinking gas, the hero doesn't hold a grudge. He uses scientific devices to remove the bug's radioactive enhancements before setting him loose in the garden. "Go ahead, little fella," he coos, "crawl away! It wasn't your fault you became radioactive! It was just a strange quirk of fate." What would comics be without those?

VS

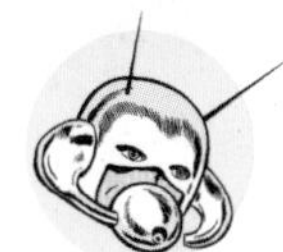

Enemy of:
Ant-Man

Created by:
Stan Lee, Larry Lieber, and Jack Kirby

Debuted in:
Tales to Astonish vol. 1, #339 (Marvel Comics, January 1963)

Not to be confused with:
The Blue Beetle (any of them)

DAY OF THE DEATH-DRONES!
CHAPTER 2
WHERE THERE'S SMOKE...
HONEST, BOSS-- WE HAD NO IDEA WE WERE FOLLOWED!
OBVIOUSLY-- BUT YOU WERE! AND IF OUR OPERATION HAS BEEN DISCOVERED BY ONE SUPER-TYPE, THERE MAY BE OTHERS!
WE CAN'T TAKE CHANCES! BRET JACKSON MUST THROW THE RACE!
LOSE ON PURPOSE? BOSS, HE'LL NEVER GO FOR IT! OUR PLAN IS WORKING, BECAUSE THE KID CAN'T SEE WHAT'S HAPPENING TO HIM! ONE BAD HABIT LEADS TO ANOTHER...
GROSS UGLY MUTANT FREAKS!! RUN! GET OUT OF HERE WHILE YOU CAN! GO! THE WORLD HAS GONE CRAZY!
ARE YOU REALLY GOING TO LEAVE YOUR LITTLE SISTER ALONE AND DEFENSELESS?
JUST IMAGINE ALL THE HORRIBLE THINGS WE COULD DO TO HER.
Oh, GOD! WHAT SHOULD I DO?
ARMOR AND STREAK
MEGALITH
YOU'RE MINE, LAWBREAKER!..
...NO ONE ESCAPES

PART 3

The MODERN AGE 1970–PRESENT

FROM THE 1970s ONWARD, AMERICAN culture embraced the antihero—with gusto. Characters like Clint Eastwood's Dirty Harry and Charles Bronson's Paul Kersey in *Death Wish* seemed to represent a peculiar, emerging breed of good guy: violent, dangerous, and only slightly better than the bad guys they punished.

Comics embraced these suddenly prominent archetypes in terrific numbers. And as the heroes grew seedier and quicker to use deadly force, the villains had to amp up their own game—sometimes with unpredictable results. More than a few hyperviolent villains became so beloved that by popular demand they joined the side of the heroes they once battled—bringing guns, knives, and a bad attitude along with them.

In many ways, a sizable chunk of the Modern Age supervillain roster represents a return to the original incarnation of the comic book baddie. Like the primogenitors of their larcenous lineage, contemporary villains kill indiscriminately in increasingly flamboyant ways, pledging themselves to evil for evil's sake. To their advantage, however, they continue the Silver Age tradition of having often-sympathetic backstories. In this fashion Modern Age comics have given us, among others, an aggrieved Uzi-toting criminal clown and a chicken-headed superhuman with a radical political agenda.

Grim, gross, and armed to the teeth, the bad guys of the most recent comic book epoch represent a relatively gruesome era in the field of supervillainy. From revived Nazis to psychedelic super-hippies, it seemed every one of them wanted to rack up a good-sized body count. But, to be fair, this era has also given us a criminal made out of bees.

THE BOG BEAST

"I have come to study the world! Why should I be feared?"

VS

Enemy of:
Humanity

Created by:
Gabriel Levy and Badia Romero

Debuted in:
Weird Tales of the Macabre #2 (Atlas-Seaboard Publications, March 1975)

Quality:
Bog standard

COMIC BOOKS HAVE ALWAYS enjoyed a good muck-monster. In 1942, a World War I German flying ace emerged from the swamp where the burning wreckage of his plane still smoldered, transformed into a shaggy mass of monstrous vegetation called the Heap. And swamp creatures have been a *thing* ever since. Most notably in the form of Marvel Comics's Man-Thing and DC Comics's Swamp Thing. Less notably, Atlas-Seaboard's blood-colored variation on the theme: the Bog Beast!

The Bog Beast belies his name just a smidge. He emerged from the La Brea tar pits rather than a marsh or swamp. Likewise, he's not so much a beast as he is an ill-prepared ambassador from a subterranean society of freaked-out-looking monster dudes.

Yes, the Bog Beast represents a hidden underworld culture, eager to explore the surface-dwelling society they long ago abandoned. To that end, the mute creature shambles around attempting to make sense of the seemingly meaningless upper world . . . and in the process tends to accidentally terrify people, or knock them around mercilessly, in his misguided attempts to merely *understand*. He innocently destroys a movie studio, slaps around a bunch of cops, *kills a beautiful werewolf,* smashes a Plymouth, takes on the United States Army . . . and flings an actor through a wall while declaring to himself, "He will be taught that all have a right to live!" (If the victim lives, he might even take the lesson to heart.)

Luckily for the Bog Beast, he has more going for him than tremendous strength, a curious intellect, and looking like a wadded-up pile of yarn coated with boiling ketchup. Bullets pass through him harmlessly, even on the several occasions where he's shot through the head and chest.

But the creature's ill-fated expedition into the modern world (that is, the modern world of 1975) ends with a whimper. Defending himself from the aforementioned werewolf, he's surprised to discover that its corpse changes before his rheumy eyes into a beautiful young woman. That's when the police descend en masse, finally capturing him in a mass of strong nets.

"Alone . . . friendless . . . DOOMED!" declares the text. But despite the "Continued . . ." caption, the story of the Bog Beast never was. It was poor sales that killed the beast.

ATLAS COMICS

APPROVED BY THE COMICS CODE AUTHORITY

NO.2 APR 43387

25¢

TALES of EVIL

FEATURING

THE BOG BEAST

GASP! I WARNED BRUNO NOT TO TAUNT THE BEAST! I *WARNED* HIM!

NOW THE MONSTER IS *FREE!*--AND EVEN *BULLETS* CAN'T STOP HIM! *NOTHING* CAN!

REVENGERS
NO. 3
$2.00 US
$2.95 CAN
Continuity Comics
STARRING
ARMOR
AND
THE SILVER STREAK
MEGALITH
YOU'RE MINE, LAWBREAKER!..
...NO ONE ESCAPES FROM
CAPTAIN LAW!

CAPTAIN LAW

"Captain Law takes no orders! Captain Law gives orders! Captain Law IS the law!"

LAW AND ORDER, TAKEN to their extremes, can be just as bad, or even worse, than outright villainy. This fact is certainly the lesson to be taken from the adventures of Captain Law (and his trusty sidekicks, Sergeant Order and Corporal Justice).

Decked out in ultrapatriotic, high-tech uniforms and piloting heavily armed and armored flying vehicles, the mustachioed captain and his pals deliver destructive force and authority on anyone they perceive to be criminals. This is a fine strategy in his initial debut, when his trio attacks and disarms a boatfull of waterborne drug smugglers. Deliberately sinking their boat and leaving them to be eaten by sharks is possibly just a little too extreme.

Still, *extreme* was Captain Law's writ. Originally Brian Farnum, a border cop renowned for his brutality, the soon-to-be Captain and his assistants form a team after Farnum is ejected from the force resulting from accusations of excessive violence and outright murder. The three men use stolen military hardware to transform themselves into the ultimate upholders of the law.

"Brian had discovered a nearly abandoned storage depot that the army had built," explains one of the Captain's henchmen. "Filled with experimental weapons . . . prototypes of top secrets. Weapons not yet finalized. Weird weapons that the army didn't trust . . . piles and piles of incredible weaponry!" So, in other words, *weapons*.

Pledging to form an independent police force not beholden to politicians, the newly christened Captain Law takes his unreasonable interpretations of right to fatal extremes. In one case, the Captain visits a spontaneous death sentence on a confrontational army general. "Incompetence is beneath the contempt of the law," he declares, atomizing the officer with a blast from his ray gun. "The punishment for incompetence is death!"

Not that Captain Law's hands are particularly clean. In a clear ends-justify-the-means-type scenario, we learn that the funding for his "extra-national" efforts are the result of running guns to warring nations.

When the Captain and his cronies mistake the Revengers (Armor, Silver Streak, and Megalith) for an invading alien force, they respond with the excess force you'd expect. Fortunately the young trio defeats the Captain as well as his Sergeant and Corporal.

"You see," growls the Captain at the end of his debut, "that's just one more reason for me to track down those aliens and grind them to the slimy pulp they're made of!" He hasn't done it yet.

VS

Enemy of:
The Revengers

Created by:
Neal Adams

Debuted in:
The Revengers featuring Megalith #3 (Continuity Comics, November 1986)

No relation to:
Marshal Law; Mr. Justice; Judge Dredd

DOOMSTALKER

"Be wise—leave this task to a being superior to you!"

Enemy of:
The Brute

Created by:
Gary Friedrich and Alan Weiss

Debuted in:
The Brute #3 (Atlas-Seaboard Comics, July 1975)

Not to be confused with:
Dr. Doom; the Night Stalker; a celery stalk

OOMSTALKER'S SOLE APPEARANCE WAS in the final issue of *The Brute*, a comic published by 1970s upstart Atlas Comics (called Atlas-Seaboard by most aficionados). For three issues, *The Brute* followed the adventures of its prehistoric, blue-skinned protagonist.

For the most part, the Brute himself was guileless and innocent. When riled, however, he became a legitimate menace (plus he definitely killed and possibly ate at least one *human child*). With that in mind, it's not surprising that forces would gather to cage or destroy him. Among them was shaggy, wild-eyed Doctor Rolf Hendrick. "The United States Defense Department! HAH!" he spits. "A more apt title would be the Department of Defeat!" That cutting wit has been unleashed because Doc's cybernetic super-soldier was rejected by the military owing to "one tiny malfunction."

But Dr. Hendrick sees an opportunity: The Brute has taken refuge upon a wrecking ball high above the ground. With police and workmen surrounding the scene, the doctor sends his cyber-warrior into play. At first, Doomstalker—despite his outré appearance and ominous name—seems to play the super*hero*. "I can halt your enemy," he tells the assembled policemen, "and there will be no risk to your lives! I ask only the opportunity to *save* lives!"

Unfortunately, he experiences a major mood swing almost immediately. "You cannot stop me," he informs the same officers, "as you will soon learn!"

Doomstalker confronts the Brute upon the wrecking ball, leading to one of the most absurd exchanges ever uttered with any seriousness in any comic book. As the Brute claims dominion over his perch by screaming "MY BALL!" Doomstalker replies "No, you poor, ignorant brute! The ball is mine—as all else upon the Earth will be!"

A terrific battle is undertaken, and Doomstalker smack-talks his way through every second of it. "Piteous creature" he barks, "though your strength is beyond a normal human's, it is useless against power such as mine!" One electronic eye zap later, the Brute plummets to the ground.

Posed triumphantly on the wrecking ball, Doomstalker jeers at the assembled crowd. "There, officers of the law! I have done your job for you!" He adds "I demand compensation!" (Said compensation being obedience to Doomstalker under threat of destruction.) Unfortunately, *The Brute* was cancelled, and Atlas-Seaboard collapsed soon thereafter, precluding any resolution to this cliffhanger. So, like Doomstalker on that wrecking ball, we're all left hanging.

ATLAS COMICS

NO. 3 JULY 43377 25c

THE BRUTE

YOU ARE DOOMED, BRUTE!

NO ONE CAN WITHSTAND THE DEATH-GAZE OF DOOMSTALKER!

CAVEMAN vs CYBORG IN "LIVE OR LET DIE"

the Heckler
2
OCT 92
US $1.25
CAN $1.50
UK 60p
COVER BLURB!
BY TOM & MARY BIERBAUM, KEITH GIFFEN AND MALCOLM JONES III

THE GENERIC MAN

"SOMETHING SAID BY THE GENERIC MAN."

THE CHAOTIC, CONTESTED BURG of Delta City is a place that, it's true, can use a little cleaning up. Crowded, dirty, and hectic as any great city, it's also saddled with colorful criminals of an almost limitless variety, held in check only by the selfless actions of the superheroic Heckler!

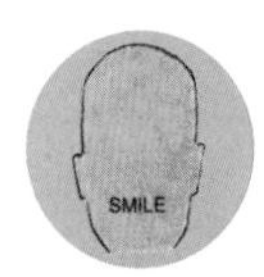

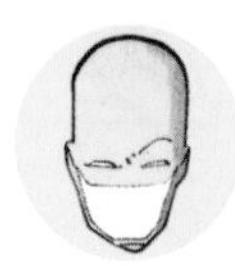

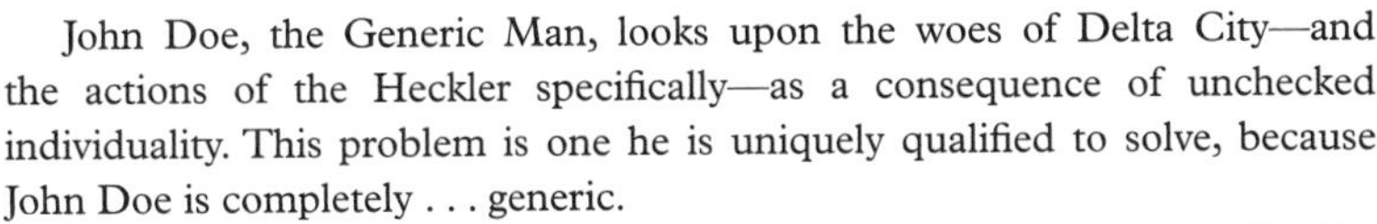

John Doe, the Generic Man, looks upon the woes of Delta City—and the actions of the Heckler specifically—as a consequence of unchecked individuality. This problem is one he is uniquely qualified to solve, because John Doe is completely . . . generic.

Depicted with a featureless pink head and hands jutting from an all-white suit, Doe expresses his intent and emotions only through the presence of sans serif type displayed on his face: "FROWN" when he's upset, "PONDER" when he's concentrating, "GLEE" when he's delighted, and so on. Likewise, Doe's mere touch can translate his genericized quality to objects, people, and animals. A newspaper in his hands becomes a white rectangle bearing only the semibold word "HEADLINE."

By means of this power the reclusive Generic Man realizes he can "save" the city, though even his dialog has a blank, generic quality to it: "I am unable to control my displeasure, considering the impact the Heckler's example could have on Delta City," he says of the hero's rampant individuality.

Realizing he can't touch every person in the city, Doe comes up with another tactic: taking a bath in the city reservoir. With his genericizing touch infecting the water supply, every living creature who comes in contact with it is replaced by an undetailed figure bearing the name of their identity: SHEEP, PEDESTRIAN, CAT, and so forth.

But soon the vigilante Minx, mob triggermen Kriegler and Ratchet-Jaw, and the heroic Heckler are bearing down on Doe's location, determined to preserve their own peculiar identities. They quickly collide in their efforts to stop the Generic Man from turning Delta City into a peaceful, delineated, and indistinguishable collection of labels.

It's Minx who puts down Doe, lethally, despite the Heckler's best efforts to intervene. It's not all over for Doe, though. As his pale, blank corpse lies on the grass, the word "DEAD" emblazoned across his chest slowly transforms into the word "REINCARNATED," and somewhere a doctor delivers a strange-looking baby whose touch turns the obstetrician's green surgical gloves a featureless white . . .

Enemy of:
A superhero

Created by:
A comic book writer

Debuted in:
A comic book

Additional blurb:
Humorous phrase

(In fact, the Generic Man was created by Keith Giffen and debuted in *The Heckler* #2; DC Comics, October 1992.)

THE NINETY-NINE

"Most of our brethren still remain trapped in their human form . . . we need to free them from their flesh prisons."

Enemy of:
Trinity Angels

Created by:
Kevin Maguire

Debuted in:
Trinity Angels #1 (Acclaim Comics, July 1997)

Number that actually showed up:
A few dozen or so

NUMBERS ARE POPULAR FOR supervillain teamnames: There's been a Terrible Trio, a Frightful Four, a Fatal Five, a Sinister Six, a Salem's Seven, and evil organizations so well staffed that they called themselves the 100 and the 1000!

When sisters Maria, Gianna, and Teresa Barbella are granted new powerful forms as the Trinity Angels, they're pitted against a small army of grotesque horrors. Ninety-nine horrors, to be specific; "social gremlins" imprisoned within powerful ancient "Trinity Gems." As the Angels' mentor explains it, every legend about gods or mythological creatures can be traced to the actions of the Ninety-Nine.

Given the gutter humor appellations and gross-out powers of the Ninety-Nine, however, it seems unlikely that they were in fact ancient inspirations of myth. What role a living mass of nasal mucus calling itself Boogieman might have played in the great mythologies of major civilizations is not only undocumented, it's patently unclear. Although not all ninety-nine of the Ninety-Nine turned up in the series, those who did make an appearance include Trenchmouth (who can eject corrosive vomit from his mouth) and his eel-like, fanged partner Rubberneck. Then there was Tongue Lasher, whose powerful, elastic tongue failed to save him in battle.

Among the rest are such relatively modest, pun-based villains as the scaly Dragonfly and the two-headed Twin Bill. More risqué puns are saved for the armored, spiked Prick (master of the "propelling pricks of vengeance"), the head-butting Head Butt, and Blowhard, a rotund gasbag who advises one hero: "That powerful wind blast of mine? It doesn't only come out the front!"

Rounding out the liberated demons were the Lord of the Fleas, the Siamese Fighting Fish, Lounge Lizard, the Diseased Squirrel (his power: "I unnerve people"), and the literally named Big Mean Monkey Head. Plus the multifunctional Mad Cow: From his udders (and why does a male cow have udders, exactly?), he is capable of squirting milks of different offensive capabilities, including stinky, sticky, and crazy milk, the last of which causes panic and madness.

Ultimately, the Trinity Angels end the Ninety-Nine's bid for power. This is a great accomplishment for justice, but a genuine loss to the world of juvenile puns. (Note: The Ninety-Nine shouldn't be confused with the Teshkeel Comics superhero title of the same name, featuring a veritable armada of heroes whose powers were inspired by the ninety-nine attributes of Allah.)

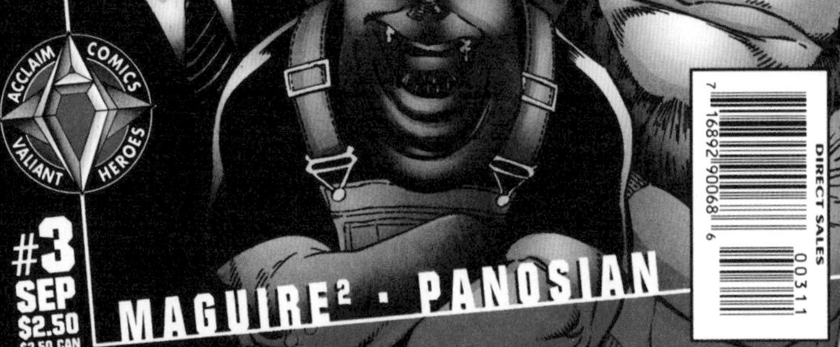
WHAT?!
WERE YOU EXPECTING SOME MORE GRATUITOUS T&A?!
ACCLAIM COMICS VALIANT HEROES
DIRECT SALES
#3
SEP
$2.50
$3.50 CAN
MAGUIRE² · PANOSIAN

POWERHOUSE

"You'll have to contend with me . . . POWERHOUSE!"

SOME VILLAINS HAVE ALL the makings of a good hero: a tormented youth, a great destiny, a secret power. Then again, sometimes they have the head of a chicken, which throws everything out of whack.

Such is the fate of Denny Atlas, a bullied and tragic young man gifted with the mantle of ancient power. Orphaned at a young age, the one thing Denny inherits from his now-deceased family is the unseen voice that drove them all to suicide. Unlike the rest of them, however, scrawny Denny listens to the voice and follows its instructions, eventually discovering an enchanted domino mask. When he dons it, he inherits the power of his direct ancestor, the sun god Ra, and becomes Powerhouse!

Why he developed a poultrylike punim is unexplained, but it's apparently part and parcel of the superpowered gig. Looking for all the world like a 'roided-out Super-Chicken, Powerhouse aligns himself with a number of other superpowered villains in the city of Chicago. Unlike the others, however, Powerhouse has slightly noble intentions: he wants to protect "super-freaks" from the scorn and prejudice of normal humans.

"We've all been ridiculed" he explains to his opponent, the Savage Dragon, during an explosive free-for-all. "But rather than become sideshow attractions for gawking, slack-jawed yokels, we've joined forces. We have power—and we use it." As he sees it, mistreatment by normal people is what's forced him and his peers into a life of crime, and if they have to use intimidation to claim respect, so be it.

Powerhouse's high ideals allow him to cross sides every now and again, on some occasions opposing the Dragon and sometimes fighting alongside him or in his place. At one point, Powerhouse even joins forces with the S.O.S., a government-funded superhero team. Will he end up as a true hero . . . or stay the villain? Only time will tell.

VS

Enemy of:
Savage Dragon

Created by:
Erik Larsen

Debuted in:
Savage Dragon #24 (Image Comics, December 1995)

Available in:
Regular;
Extra Crispy

THE ROACH WRANGLER

"We leave at midnight. Every roach in the city of Chicago . . ."

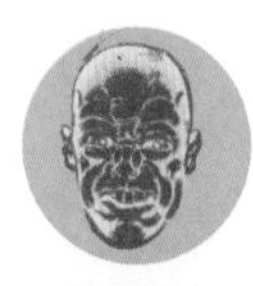

Enemy of:
The Badger

Created by:
Mike Baron and Bill Reinhold

Debuted in:
The Badger #27 (First Comics, September 1987)

Not to be confused with:
Wrangler Roach, cowboy vermin (who does not exist . . . yet)

CONSIDERING THAT THEY'RE ONE of the most problematic, hated, and reviled household pests, it's kind of surprising that cockroaches haven't inspired more comic book villains. One of the select few is the Roach Wrangler, whose powers and appearance are as gross as the name implies.

Answering to slumlord Elmo Zims (who bears an uncanny resemblance to musician Fats Waller), the Roach Wrangler is employed to coerce Chicago's plentiful cockroach population into helping Zims clear his property of troublesome tenants. Curious about his partner in crime, Zims asks the Roach Wrangler to explain how he gained the power to control the cockroach.

"I was a pest control officer with the U.S. Information Agency in the Sudan," the villain recounts. "I was lost in a sandstorm and fell into a pit. It was the entrance to an undiscovered Egyptian tomb. I lay trapped for thirty days. I had nothing to eat or drink . . . but the roaches. *An endless parade straight into my mouth.* I knew I was changing. I could not help myself."

Settle your stomach as the Wrangler goes on to describe how, after his month spent trapped in the hidden tomb, he was given a gift by his skittering roommates: a golden, roach-shaped wand. "From that day forth they have danced to my tune," he says.

The Roach Wrangler has designs on ruling Chicago as its undisputed roach king. But he comes into conflict with Wisconsin's resident costumed vigilante the Badger, a martial artist with multiple personalities and a seemingly supernatural connection to the animal kingdom. At the Illinois-Wisconsin state line, two armies converge. On the Roach Wrangler's side, "one billion roaches make a noise like fat sizzling on a white hot griddle—amplified beyond the threshold of pain."

On the Badger's side, however, is a repelling force of steamrollers, road graders, trained elephants, horses, rats, cats, and dogs. At his rallying cry of "GOOSH! GOOSH FOR ALL YOU'RE WORTH," the Badger and his forces demolish the roaches, reducing the swarming masses to a paste suitable only for lawn fertilizer.

As for the Roach Wrangler, his popularity surges. With Chicago having been depleted of its troublesome cockroach population, other cities seek to employ him as a pied piper of pests. He fails to take the offer, preferring to occasionally return for more roach-related criminality. Still, it must be nice to have a career to fall back on.

MARVEL® COMICS GROUP
SPIDER-MAN STORM and POWER MAN
BATTLE SMOKESCREEN!

SMOKESCREEN

"Soon enough, the world shall hear of the man called Smokescreen!"

UPERHERO COMICS ARE TRADITIONALLY the realm of the morality play. Heroes and villains are pitted against one another as clearly defined defenders of good and proponents of evil. At its extreme, this easily comprehensible model of wrong versus right makes a great template for a whole subgenre of comics.

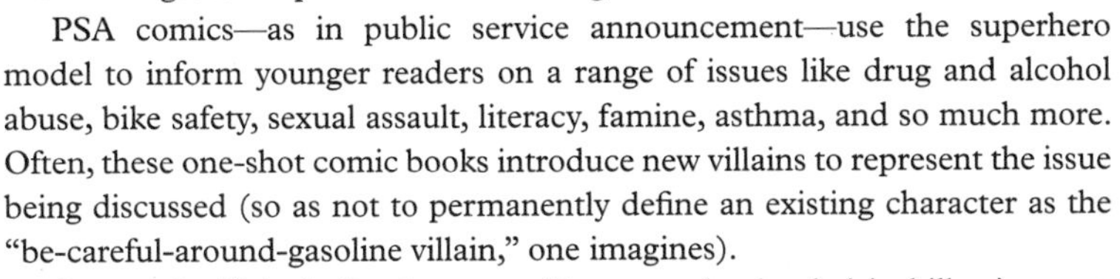

PSA comics—as in public service announcement—use the superhero model to inform younger readers on a range of issues like drug and alcohol abuse, bike safety, sexual assault, literacy, famine, asthma, and so much more. Often, these one-shot comic books introduce new villains to represent the issue being discussed (so as not to permanently define an existing character as the "be-careful-around-gasoline villain," one imagines).

One such villain is Smokescreen. Permanently clouded in billowing grey smoke like some sort of insidious version of Pigpen from *Peanuts* and decked out in a black-and-orange costume with smoke-emblazoned highlights, he's a high-stakes gambler with an eye toward controlling the mob sports-betting scene. (Other symbolic villains who populated PSA comics include the Asthma Monster, the illiterate Trog, and Vapora, aka the Fume of Doom, a living embodiment of dangerous, unchecked gasoline vapor.)

Smoking is only his tool in achieving his larger dreams. Luring a promising young track star named Bret Jackson to his cigarette-stocked youth center, Smokescreen and his cronies ply the boy with the rich flavor of top-tier tobacco. This naturally reduces Bret's athleticism . . . which somehow requires the efforts of three superheroes to investigate. While the book rightly outlines many of the health issues associated with smoking, it does stretch credulity a bit when it implies that tobacco will also get you involved with criminals who threaten you into throwing high-stakes sporting events.

The combined efforts of Spider-Man, Luke Cage (aka Power Man), and Storm (from the X-Men) put Smokescreen down for the count, although they're too late to help Bret Jackson win the big meet. Smoking ruined his cardiovascular system for this season, and returning to his previous championship levels will take training. Hopefully he won't run into any supervillains trying to stuff him full of drugs, fatty foods, or indolence.

Enemy of:
Spider-Man, Storm, and Power Man

Created by:
John Romita and an uncredited writer

Debuted in:
Spider-Man, Storm, and Power Man custom publication (Marvel Comics, June, 1982)

Weakness:
"No Smoking" signs

SWARM

"Through me, they create—they think! Through them, I live . . . and conquer!"

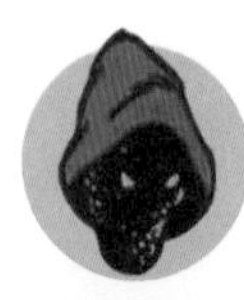

Enemy of:
The Champions, Spider-Man, etc.

Created by:
Bill Mantlo and John Byrne

Debuted in:
Champions #14 (Marvel Comics, July 1977)

Friends call him:
"Honeybunch," "Buzzy," "Drone"

TWO FACTS ARE VERY true of comic book super-characters: You can't go wrong with bees. And you'll never find a better villain than a Nazi. These axioms are evident in hundreds—if not thousands—of comic books. But they've never come together quite as decisively as with Swarm, the man made of Nazi bees!

In fact, Swarm represented a concatenation of two popular media-driven fears of his late-'70s era: an invasion of South American "killer" bees, and a hidden menace of relocated Nazis inhabiting those south-of-the-border jungles. If only Swarm were also disco-themed, he'd have been the era's ultimate triple-threat.

The would-*bee* world conqueror is Fritz von Meyer, "world expert on toxic poisons, apiculturalist, and expatriate Nazi!" In an unnamed South American nation, he hides from Nazi-hunting Interpol agents and wiles away the hours studying the breeding patterns of killer bees. His life sounds almost idyllic.

Hiking the jungle trails, von Meyer stumbles across a strange, huge hive of passive bees he's never before encountered. Suspecting the bees were mutated by radioactive meteors, von Meyer unwisely blasts the insects with additional radiation. His intent is to reawaken their killer instincts and find a way to control them: the first steps in organizing the normally sedate bees into a word-conquering army.

Predictably enough, the ray backfires. The bees reacquire their reputed viciousness and then some, attacking and stinging von Meyer en masse. Until he grasps the queen bee! Somehow this grants Fritz the power to replace his irreparably stung body with that of an intelligent bee swarm. He becomes, as he puts it, "a living embodiment of the swarm."

An assault on Los Angeles brings the attention of the Champions, a short-lived super-team so irrelevant to the Marvel universe that the parent company barely noticed when the trademark lapsed. Now-famous film stars Black Widow and Ghost Rider, plus immortal Greek god Hercules, former X-Men Iceman and Angel, and their Russian cohort Darkstar, confront Swarm and his army (which now includes giant robot bees, inexplicably).

All seems lost. Until the powerfully strong Hercules saves the day by hurling the hypothyroidal queen bee—roughly the size of a Volkswagen Beetle—over the ocean. The bees of Swarm's mass follow, leaving the Nazi apiarist a collapsed heap of bones. Swarm returned to menace other Marvel superheroes, but his initial ignoble defeat must have surely, truly . . . stung.

MARVEL® COMICS GROUP

PETER PARKER, THE SPECTACULAR SPIDER-MAN®

MICHAEL NASSER & JOE RUBINSTEIN

INTO THE HIVE!

BEEN SHOT!
ANOTHER JINGLER MURDER!
COME ON, ROY!
THE JINGLER LEFT HIS CALLING CARD, A JINGLE!
WE'RE TOO LATE-HE'S BEEN MURDERED!
SO FAR THE JINGLER'S VICTIMS ARE ALL PUBLISHERS, ROY!
THAT'S SOME-THING TO WORK ON, WIZARD!
MR. STRUNK I BELIEVE!
WHAT DO YOU WANT?
THE JINGLER'S NEXT VICTIM, SIMEON STRUNK, PUBLISHER--
YOUR LIFE!
BANG

12¢
PATRO
THEY'RE TRAPPED-- AND I CAN'T HELP THEM BECAUSE THE SWAMP IS SWALLOWING UP MY ROBOT BODY!

APPROVED BY THE COMICS CODE AUTHORITY
133 JAN
CAPTAIN AMERICA
THE POWER OF-- BULLDOZER
EXTRA! THE ORIGIN OF MODOK!

THEN SUDDENLY... OUT OF THE NIGHT SKY...
KRANG!
I AM IN CHARGE OF THIS OPERATION, SOLDIER. AND I'D LIKE TO KNOW JUST WHAT BRANCH OF THE ARMED SERVICES YOU BELONG TO, AND WHAT YOU'RE DOING HERE?!!
I AM CAPTAIN LAW! MY JURISDICTION IS ALL EXTRA-NATIONAL LAW!
ALIENS ARE EXTRA NATIONAL!
MY MEN AND I HAVE BEEN MONITORING YOUR CLOSED-CIRCUIT RADIO!
YOUR HANDLING OF THIS SITUATION IS INEFFICIENT, AND SLOPPY!

THESE ALIENS WILL BE TAKEN INTO CUSTODY IN DUE TIME. BUT MY ORDERS ARE TO SEE THAT THEY COME TO NO HARM UNLESS THEY FORCE US TO HARM THEM.

CAPTAIN LAW TAKES NO ORDERS!

ACKNOWLEDGMENTS

The author would like to thank the Digital Comic Museum (digitalcomicmuseum.com) and Comic Book Plus (comicbookplus.com), without whose tireless archivists and exhaustive catalog the research for the majority of this book would have been impossible.

Much gratitude goes out to the work of the late Don Markstein, as well as Jess Nevins, Les Daniels, Ron Goulart, Gerard Jones, and many others.

Additional thanks to everyone who visits and comments at my comics blogs, *Gone & Forgotten* and *The Chronological Superman*.

And lastly, thanks to everyone at Quirk Books!

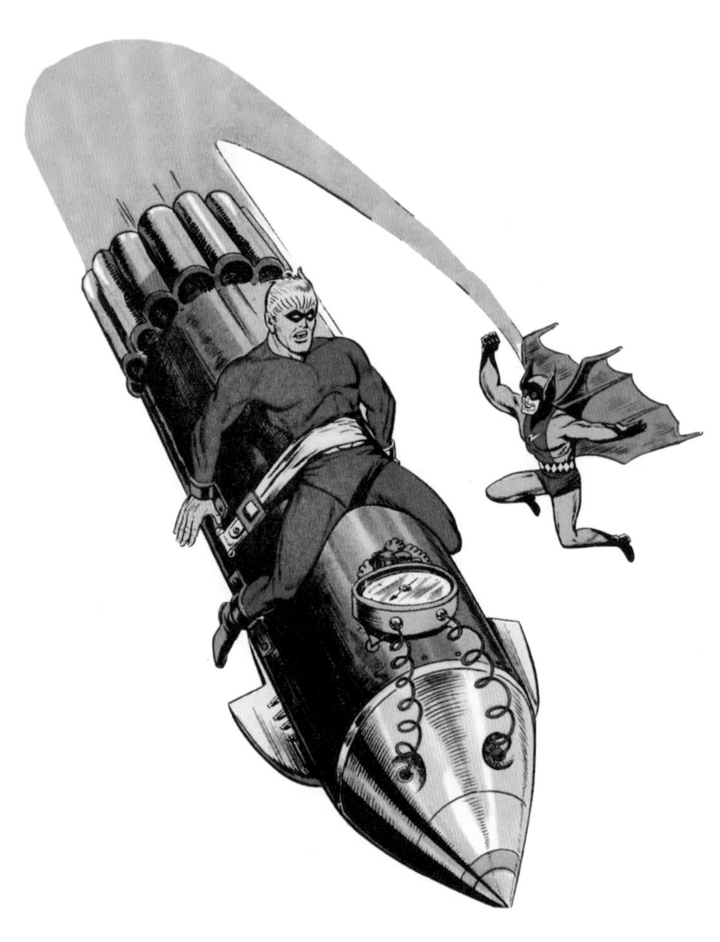